Peace and Stability in Rwanda and Burundi: The Road Not Taken

Godfrey Mwakikagile

Peace and Stability in Rwanda and Burundi:
The Road Not Taken

First Edition

ISBN 978-9987-16-032-7

New Africa Press
Dar es Salaam, Tanzania

Printed in the United Kingdom

29°
30°
31°
Uganda
Rutshuru
Kisoro
Kabale
Kagitumba R.
Dem. Rep. of Congo
Ruhengeri
Lac Burera
Lac Rwanye
Byumba
Mukungwa R.
Goma
Gisenyi
Rwanda
Lac Ihema
Lac Kivu
Kigali
Lac Muhazi
2°
Kalehe
Kibuye
Gitarama
Kibungo
Mwogo R.
Gikongoro
Rweru
Cyangugu
Luhwa R.
Cohoha
Kirundo
Ruwa R.
Butare
Tanzania
Cibitoke
Ngozi
Muyinga
Kayanza
3°
Ruvubu R.
Bubanza
Karuzi
Muramvya
Cankuzo
Ruvironza R.
Ruvubu R.
Uvira
Bujumbura
Gitega
Ruyigi
Kibondo
Burundi
Rutana
Lake Tanganyika
4°
Bururi
0 150 km
0 100 mi
Makamba
Fizi
©1997 MAGELLAN Geographix℠
(805) 685-3100 www.maps.com

Introduction

THIS work looks at some of the ways to achieve lasting peace and stability in Rwanda and Burundi whose destiny is inextricably linked with the entire Great Lakes region of East Africa.

Conflicts in the two countries affect the entire region, especially their neighbours – Tanzania, Congo, and Uganda – and have ripple effects which go far beyond the region.

Therefore all the countries in the region have direct interest in what goes on in Rwanda and Burundi and in the resolution of the conflicts in the twin nations.

But resolution of the conflict between the Hutu and the Tutsi in Rwanda and Burundi may require a solution that has never been tried before. It may even require a combination of solutions in order to be resolved permanently.

Any solution, however radical, should be tried even if it runs counter to the logic of what African leaders and many other Africans consider to be the proper way to build nations and achieve unity transcending racial, ethnic and regional differences.

Resolution of the conflict in Rwanda and Burundi may also provide some insights into the complexities of conflict management, and conflict resolution, in other intra-territorial and regional conflicts and disputes in other parts of the continent.

Of paramount importance should be the courage, determination, and willingness of Africans to take bold initiatives and make dynamic compromises to resolve conflicts even if it means abolishing the boundaries inherited at independence and redrawing the map of Africa, even if it means allowing some groups or regions to secede, and even if it means partitioning some countries to achieve lasting peace and stability.

Rwanda and Burundi may provide a template for that if the people of those two countries decide to use innovative solutions to resolve their conflict which, probably more than anything else, is waged along ethnic lines to the detriment of African unity and solidarity.

Part One:

A War That May Never End

PROSPECTS for peace in the Great Lakes region remained bleak at best as fighting continued through the years after the Rwandan genocide.

Congo was embroiled in its own conflict which drew in several neighbours: Rwanda, Uganda, Burundi, Sudan, and Angola. Zimbabwe, Namibia, and Chad, which don't even border Congo, also entered the war.

The civil war between the Hutu and the Tutsi in Burundi intensified, forcing more than 5,000 people to flee everyday into neighbouring Tanzania since January 2000.

Rwanda was still locked in a brutal war of attrition between the Hutu and the Tutsi.

Uganda also had to contend with its own insurgents operating within the country and others using Congo and

Sudan as launching pads for their raids into Ugandan border regions and beyond.

But it was the ethnic conflict between the Hutu and the Tutsi in Rwanda and Burundi which was at the centre of this regional imbroglio. It posed the biggest threat to long-term peace and stability in East-Central Africa and had the potential to draw in other countries as it continued to go on.

And it was the ethnic conflict in Rwanda which led to the downfall of President Mobutu Sese Seko of Zaire when it spilled over into his country. The conflict in Congo eventually escalated into an international war involving nine countries during the presidency of Laurent Kabila when the leaders of Rwanda, Uganda and Burundi invaded his country in support of the rebels trying to overthrow him.

Therefore the war in Congo was inextricably linked with the perennial conflicts in both Rwanda and Burundi. And Hut rebels continued to use eastern Congo as an operational base for their military campaign against the two Tutsi-dominated states.

The campaign spread terror throughout the Great Lakes region, sending waves of refugees across borders – back and forth, depending on the level of violence – in a migratory pattern that became a permanent feature of the region's political landscape.

This kind of nomadic existence for Hutus and Tutsis – reminiscent of the plight of the Palestinian refugees – has been going on since 1959 when a mass uprising by the Hutu forced hundreds of thousands of Tutsis to flee Rwanda and seek refuge in neighbouring countries.

About 400,000 of them eventually settled in Uganda which had the largest number of Tutsi refugees in the region who fled Rwanda in 1959 and in the 1960s.

The level of violence rose sharply in the 1960s, forcing countless refugees, mostly Hutu, to flee both Rwanda and Burundi and seek sanctuary in Tanzania and Congo.

8

Reign of Terror:
A Tale of Three Nations

When hundreds of thousands of Hutu refugees returned to Rwanda from Zaire and Tanzania towards the end of 1996, thousands of Hutu militants – who were among the perpetrators of the 1994 genocide – refused to go back with them.

Most of the Hutu extremists remained in Zaire and continued to wage war against the Tutsi-dominated Rwandan Patriotic Army (RPA). But many others also returned to their homeland together with the civilian refugees whom they used as a cover to slip back into Rwanda.

Since August 1997, they stepped up their campaign within Rwanda and from their bases in Congo (as Zaire was renamed in May 1997), threatening full-scale war against the Tutsi-dominated regime in which thousands of people were killed: "In the past six months, militant members of the Hutu tribe...have infiltrated their homeland and massacred an estimated 5,000 people in what have become almost daily attacks."[1]

The rebels operating from their bases within Burundi also coordinated their attacks with their kinsmen in eastern Congo and Rwanda for a sustained campaign against the Tutsi in the three countries. Hundreds of people were killed in Burundi and in eastern Congo by the rebels during the same period thousands perished in the civil war in Rwanda.

Diplomats and aid workers in the embattled region said Rwandan Hutu extremists were spread throughout eastern Congo, Burundi and western Tanzania, determined to overthrow the Tutsi-controlled government in Kigali. The guerrillas were able to slip in and out of Rwanda, operating from rear bases in the three neighbouring

9

countries. They also caused security problems for those countries.

Although the conflict was basically ethnic between the Hutu and the Tutsi, it also had regional dimensions with profound implications for the entire Great Lakes region: economic dislocation and retarded growth, national disintegration, and escalation of the war across borders involving African and non-African countries.

The potential for disruption was enormous. In fact, the region had already sustained heavy damage from the war especially in the economic arena. As Seth Kamanzi, adviser to Rwandan President Pasteur Bizimungu, conceded:

"It's a regional problem. What's happening in Rwanda is connected to what's happening in eastern Congo and what's happening in Burundi. The problem must be seen in a regional context."[2]

The most volatile part was Gisenyi Province in northwestern Rwanda for two reasons. It is a fiercely independent region which provided the strongest support to the rebels. And among all the provinces of Rwanda, it was the most accessible for the insurgents from their bases across the border in eastern Congo.

In early January 1998, about 1,000 Hutu rebels invaded the province and split into highly mobile units for maximum efficiency. They went on to kill and mutilate hundreds of people in a killing frenzy that lasted for several days. The raids had a profound impact on the region and on the country as a whole, whose leaders claimed that the insurgents were not as effective as they seemed to be. The fact that they terrorised the region with impunity disproved this claim.

Neighbouring Burundi was caught in the same vicious cycle of violence which continued through the years claiming more than 200,000 lives by the end of 1999;

about 500,000 victims, mostly Hutu, within three years since October 1993, according to other sources cited by *The Economist* as we learned earlier, a genocide which was sparked by the assassination of Hutu President Melchior Ndadaye by Tutsi soldiers. The attack by Hutu rebels on 1 January 1998 was one of the most dramatic:

"On New Year's Day, Burundi Hutu – reportedly assisted by Rwandan Hutu – attacked the airport outside the capital Bujumbura, killing at least 274 people.
The size, sophistication and location of the attack alarmed officials in the region. That 1,000 Hutu could fashion a four-pronged assault on the capital's airport appeared to herald a new brazenness and brutality in Burundi's civil conflict."[3]

In spite of the brutal nature of their campaign, it is clear that the rebels had political objectives in mind; the fundamental reason being the asymmetrical relationship between the Hutu and the Tutsi based on inequality and lack of power by the Hutu. However, Rwandan government officials argued that Hutu militants had only one goal in mind: to kill as many Tutsis as possible in eastern Congo, Rwanda, and Burundi.

That is a simplistic view of a complex phenomenon deeply rooted in history.

Instead of dismissing their guerrilla campaign as sheer terrorism and as an end in itself, critics of the insurgents should address a few fundamental questions:

Why are they fighting – is it not because the Hutu majority are powerless and are dominated by the Tutsi minority?

Why didn't the Hutu in Rwanda mobilise forces before, to kill Tutsis, through the decades since independence in 1962 – until after the Tutsi-dominated Rwandan Patriotic Army (RPA) invaded the country from Uganda in October 1990?

And why did the Hutu in Burundi go to war against the Tutsi in October 1993 immediately after the assassination of the country's first democratically elected president, Melchior Ndadaye, a Hutu, who was bayoneted to death by Tutsi soldiers in an abortive coup attempt?

We have to be honest and fair to both sides. As Alison DesForges, an official of Human Rights Watch/Africa who studied Rwanda for more than 30 years, put it: "If Tutsi are being killed today, it's because these guys (the Hutu) want power." Otherwise, she went on to say, the military campaign by the Hutu "just seems totally futile."[4] And as Neil Kressel states in his book, *Mass Hate: The Global Rise of Genocide and Terror*:

"The precolonial Tutsi domination of Hutus in Rwanda...was clearly an exploitative system. When the system fell apart (beginning with the Hutu uprising in November 1999) and the exploited realized what had happened, their anger intensified.

The persistence of denigrating stereotypes (of Hutus as dim-witted, ugly, servile, submissive, lazy, stupid, and so on) added to their fury: 'They think they were born to rule; we will show them.'

Moreover, many Hutu remained psychologically fearful of returning to their former predicament (of being subjugated, oppressed and exploited by the Tutsi). When the realistic threat from the RPF (the Tutsi-dominated Rwandan Patriotic Front) appeared, it was a relatively simple matter to activate a nightmare scenario. The genocide, by this logic, had its deepest roots in a precolonial system based on a 'premise of inequality.'"[5]

The genocide did, of course, almost wipe out the entire Tutsi population of Rwanda. But the continuing civil war between the Hutu and the Tutsi, after the genocide, also had unintended consequences. Ironically, the guerrilla campaign was most destructive where it was most effective, the same region where it also had the biggest support: Gisenyi Province.

International aid workers were forced to stop development projects in the region which were desperately needed by the people whose lives had been shattered by years of conflict and economic collapse caused by the war. As Paula Ghedini of the UN High Commission for Refugees (UNHCR) said: "There was a time when some agencies were moving from relief to development. How can you talk about reintegration when people are literally under attack every day?"[6]

The attack on Hutu civilians came mostly from the Rwandan army which was mostly Tutsi. They were caught between their own people, the Hutu rebels, and the Tutsi soldiers who attacked them indiscriminately to flush out the insurgents and retaliate for the rebel attacks.

One of the most disturbing features of the rebel attacks was coordination. There was circumstantial evidence showing that the raids were well-coordinated. For instance, on 19 January 1998, 37 people were killed in Gisenyi Province in ambushes that occurred only minutes apart. According to a report from Gisenyi in the *International Herald Tribune*:

"Thirty-five of the victims were riding a company bus to their jobs at the national brewery (in the town of Gisenyi). The assailants stopped the bus, asked the workers to separate into ethnic groups – then shot Hutu and Tutsi alike and burned the bus. Hutu onlookers reportedly applauded the attack.

The next day, at least five Tutsi soldiers were found dead on the road between Gisenyi and nearby Ruhengeri Province....

Then, on Saturday (24 January 1998), eight civilians were shot and hacked to death by Hutu rebels in Ruhengeri. At the same time, at least 100 people were killed in Burundi in ethnic fighting from January 17 to 21.

In one incident, Hutu militants killed 33 people in fighting with the army the night of January 20, just south of Bujumbura."[7]

When looked at collectively, the raids spanned a vast expanse of territory, from northwestern Rwanda all the way down to its southern neighbour Burundi. And they were carried out by members of the same ethnic group, the Hutu, fighting a common enemy, the Tutsi.

What would account for such successful attacks against two seasoned armies – the Rwandan army and the Burundian army, both predominantly Tutsi – with a reputation of being some of the best on the entire continent?

The attacks on Burundi's capital, Bujumbura, also pointed to the emergence of a new phenomenon in this war, coordination by the rebels, which had been noticeably absent in previous engagements.

The attack on the Tutsi refugee camp at Mudende in northwestern Rwanda on 11 December 1997 and another raid around the same time on the town of Cyangugu in the southwestern part of the country by a combined force of Rwandan Hutu insurgents and a Congolese tribal militia known as Mai-Mai; as well as the brazenness of all the attacks including the attack on Burundi's capital, not only showed excellent coordination but also sophistication and relentless determination by the Hutu insurgents to wage war against a superior enemy who was better armed. As one official of an international relief agency working in Rwanda said: "It's very reasonable to think that all those things are linked, and that cannot be good."[8]

In spite of compelling evidence – however circumstantial – of such coordination, some people either minimised its significance or dismissed it as unrealistic. Many people including diplomats and international relief workers in the embattled region said no one really knew how well-organised the rebels were. One was Seth

14

Sendashonga, a Hutu who was Rwanda's minister of internal affairs until late 1995. He said people simply "go overboard when they talk of a coordinated plan."[9]

But it was not that simple, dismissing the attacks as un-coordinated.

Sendashonga contended that sophisticated coordination of the insurgency by the rebels in Rwanda, Congo, and Burundi was almost impossible because so many leaders of the former Rwandan Hutu national army were scattered throughout Europe and Africa – even North America – after the 1994 genocide.

Yet he himself conceded that several thousand Rwandan Hutus had teamed up with the Mai-Mai tribal militiamen in eastern Congo (the two rebel groups jointly attacked Cyangugu in December 1997), and that Burundi's Hutu insurgents had recruited their Rwandan kinsmen into their guerrilla forces.

That is a significant concession on his part, however inadvertent, that the attacks were indeed coordinated, even if not at a very high level because of the absence from the combat zone of so many military officers of the former Rwandan national army as he pointed out.

There was further evidence showing that the guerrilla campaign across national boundaries by different rebel groups was coordinated. Even diplomats and relief workers who said no one really knew how well-organised the insurgents were – about which they were right – admitted that Rwandan Hutu rebels had established close ties with other rebel groups in eastern Congo, Burundi, and Tanzania when they lived in refugee camps in those countries for more than two years.

The camps became some of the best recruiting grounds for new rebels and centres of intrigue for Hutu politicians and other members of the Hutu elite plotting against the Tutsi-dominated regime in Kigali.

Even the Zairian army under President Mobutu Sese Seko, longtime foe of the Tutsi, supported the Hutu rebels in their war against the Tutsi in eastern Zaire – where local tribes were already hostile to Zairian Tutsis – and in the two Tutsi-dominated states of Rwanda and Burundi. And after Mobutu was overthrown, remnants of his army remained staunch allies of the Hutu rebels:

"In eastern Congo, they have hooked up with members of Marshall Mobutu's former army and the Mai-Mai – both known to despise the Congolese Tutsi.
In their combined attack on December11 (1997), 500 Mai-Mai guerrillas and Rwandan Hutu crossed into southwestern Rwanda to attack the town of Cyangugu, after first attacking the border city of Bukavu (under Tutsi control) in eastern Congo."[10]

It was a well-coordinated raid.
But it was not only the rebels who coordinated their campaign from their bases in eastern Congo, Rwanda and Burundi, and from the refugee camps in western Tanzania. The Rwandan regime shared, on regular basis, intelligence information with the governments of Uganda, Congo (under President Laurent Kabila until they turned against each other in 1998), Ethiopia, Eritrea, and even Angola (until their alliance with Angola ended in 1998 when Angola started supporting Kabila) where many Hutu extremists settled and joined forces with the rebels of UNITA who were fighting to overthrow the Angolan government.
The conflict in the Great Lakes region of East-Central Africa had the largest number of armies and rebel groups and was the most internationalised war in the history of post-colonial Africa whose participants were mostly African.
Rwandan and Burundian leaders were confident that they would defeat the rebels. In fact, in 1998, Rwandan officials even predicted that they would neutralise the insurgents within months.

But that was sheer wishful thinking. Many observers believed that the rebels could terrorise the region for years unless meaningful concessions were made by the governments involved to satisfy at least some of the basic demands made by the insurgents. As the relief official in Rwanda, quoted earlier, stated: "I'm deeply pessimstic." He went on to say that if the Rwandan Hutu rebels "ever really get their act together" with other rebel groups in the region, "it would be disastrous."[11]

That was a much more realistic assessment.

The war continued, fuelled by different perceptions of the conflict by both sides.

The rebels saw it as a political struggle for the rights of the powerless Hutu majority living under brutal subjugation by the Tutsi.

The dominant Tutsi minority saw it as an attempt to exterminate them.

Tragically, both were right.

A Nation in Turmoil

The war in Rwanda continued in the late nineties in varying degrees of intensity.

It continued to be fuelled by several factors: ethnic animosity; Hutu aspirations for political and economic equality; Tutsi domination and insecurity including fear of extermination; conflicting perceptions and interests of the two ethnic groups; attempts by Hutu extremists to overthrow the Tutsi-dominated regime and exterminate the Tutsi or expel them from the country if possible; and raw ambition for power by the Hutu elite to institute a Hutu ethnocracy which, for all intents and purposes, would be no better than the Tutsi ethnocratic regime they wanted to replace.

A Hutu ethnocracy could be even worse if the militant Hutu elite were to re-establish Hutu supremacy – it existed for 32 years from 1962 to 1994 – by invoking the "natural right" of the Hutu to rule perpetually; a right ostensibly derived from their status as the numerically preponderant ethnic group but actually from tribalism and visceral hatred for the Tutsi. It is an agenda that could lead to another genocide as the final solution to the "Tutsi problem" – as defined by the Hutu elite.

It was a deadly combination of factors, compounded by the toxic politics and instability of the Great Lakes region because of the protracted conflict in Congo involving nine countries, the civil wars in Burundi and Uganda, and the refugee problem throughout the embattled region.

Rwanda was a nation in turmoil, trapped in a vicious cycle of violence. The 1994 genocide was a constant reminder of what could happen again. And its anniversaries became occasions for profound reflection on the state of the republic and its future as a unitary state – in a country where its citizens, friends and foes and alike, are united by blood, culture, history, and geography, yet so divided as if they have nothing in common.

Such was the occasion, for profound reflection, on the genocide's fourth anniversary on 8 April 1998. According to a report from Bisesero, Rwanda, in *The Boston Globe*:

"Nine wooden coffins, containing remains of some who died in the Rwandan massacre of 1994, were lowered into an unfinished crypt yesterday, in a ceremony honoring Tutsi who fought back.

When complete, the tomb will form part of a memorial to...Rwandans who were killed in massacres that began four years ago yesterday, orchestrated by the Hutu government.

Nearby, a huge pile of skulls and bones, with bits of cloth clinging to them, awaited burial. Red, green and yellow Rwandan flags flew at half-staff, flapping in the breeze.

One official representing European nations expressed remorse yesterday. 'There was a responsibility of those who did not correctly appreciate the situation....It was a mistake also when we allowed the (Hutu) refugee camps (in Zaire) to be populated by people who are now threatening Rwanda,' Aldo Ajello, who represents the 15-nation European Union (EU) in central Africa's Great Lakes region, told a crowd of several thousands gathered on a hilltop in Bisesero, in western Rwanda.

Ajello did not become the EU's representative until after the slaughter....

The European Union's expression of remorse followed President Clinton's acknowledgment in Rwanda last month that the outside world failed to take the slaughter seriously....

A portion of the memorial tomb will be dedicated to what a local official called 'international betrayal.'"[12]

The anniversary came only a few days after another wave of violence in Rwanda. On 4 April 1998, Hutu rebels launched a deadly raid in the central region and hacked seven Tutsis to death. One of the victims was a baby.[13]

As in most raids of this kind, the insurgents were armed with clubs and machetes. The timing of the raid was intended to send a strong message to the Tutsi-dominated regime that the rebels were still a factor to be reckoned with. The attack almost coincided with the anniversary observance of the 1994 genocide.

And about two weeks later, two Hutu priests were sentenced to death after a court in the Rwandan capital, Kigali, found them guilty of genocide and crimes against humanity. Jean Francois Kayiranga and Edouard Nkurikiye were the first priests to be convicted in Rwanda's genocide trial.[14] Genocide trials in Rwanda began in December 1996. The two priests were found guilty on 17 April 1998 of killing 2,000 Tutsis who sought refuge at Nyange Catholic Church in Kivumu commune, about 47 miles west of Kigali in north-central Rwanda.

In chilling testimony, the court heard that the priests ordered the demolition of the church by a mechanical digger. The Tutsi refugees trapped inside were crushed to death or buried alive in the debris. The driver of the digger, Anastase Nkinamubanzi who was paid by the priests to demolish the church, was sentenced to life imprisonment. The two priests also organised the massacre of more than 60 Tutsis at Nyundo in northwestern Rwanda. Most of the victims were priests, nuns, and seminarians.[15]

Other Hutu clergymen were among the tens of thousands of their fellow tribesmen in prisons across Rwanda awaiting trial for genocide. According to the United Nations, about 130,000 genocide suspects had been detained by April 1998.

It was the largest concentration of war crime suspects in prison in the world during that period and retained that unenviable record for many years.

As the war continued, so did the trials, many of which ended in death sentences.

One of the most memorable aspects of these trials and convictions was public execution of some of the perpetrators of the 1994 genocide. The executions were carried out in pursuit of justice. But they were also a reminder of the turmoil in that troubled land which remained deeply divided along ethnic lines, probably even more so after the holocaust. The executions only added to the polarisation. While the Tutsi saw them as the culmination of their quest for justice and warranted retribution, the Hutu saw the executions as part of a witch hunt directed against them by a racist, oppressive Tutsi-dominated regime.

Executions

Rwanda's first executions of those who received death sentences in the genocide trials took place in April 1998. A total of 116 people had been condemned to death by then. But not all were executed that month.

Justice Minister Faustin Nteziryayo announced on April 22nd that more than 20 convicts would be executed on April 24th. He said the executions would be carried out by firing squad and in public. He went on to say: "It is over 20 people. The files of other convicts who requested presidential clemency have not yet been finalized."[16] The executions were ordered at a special cabinet meeting on April 20th when President Pasteur Bizimungu, a Hutu, turned down pleas for clemency.

Members of the general public were invited to watch the executions in a soccer stadium in the nation's capital, Kigali, and at four provincial towns in different parts of Rwanda. More executions followed through the years.

Radio Rwanda quoted a cabinet statement in April 1998 which stated that the executions "will act as a lesson to people who do not respect the lives of others." It was a warning to Hutu rebels who, the government said, were "still bent on pursuing genocide."[17]

A group of holocaust survivors called the Association of Peace Volunteers hailed the decision to go on with the public executions as a just one and a deterrent: "We welcome these punishments because they will definitely do away with the culture of impunity that has damaged our country."[18]

Rwandan officials also said the executions will assure survivors of the genocide that justice had been done. As the Rwandan ambassador to the United Nations, Gideon Kayinamura, put it: "I think this will be a source of joy for all people who have suffered. It will signal that impunity cannot go unpunished."[19] he said the executions would be carried out in the towns where the crimes occurred, including the capital Kigali some of whose streets were clogged with dead bodies after a massacre of tens of thousands of Tutsis and many Hutu moderates in the city. At least 60,000 people perished in Kigali alone.

But the decision to execute the convicted criminals drew criticism from legal experts and human rights advocates who contended that Rwanda's judicial system was deeply flawed, unable to dispense justice. As Peter Takirambudde, a spokesman for the New York-based Human Rights Watch, said: "There was no due process. The initial trials clearly did not approximate anything which would be consistent with due process. Rwanda has a long way to go in developing an impartial and credible and effective justice system."[20] And a UN human rights official in Kigali, Jose Luis Herrero, said: "The UN protests the carrying out of the executions."[21]

But Rwandan officials ignored the protests and proceeded with the executions. They rejected worldwide pleas for clemency, and some people, mostly Tutsi, who barely escaped the massacres, said they would be there to watch. An urgent appeal from Pope John Paul II to Rwandan officials for clemency was also dismissed outright by the authorities in Kigali. Minister of State Patrick Mazimhaka was blunt in his response: "We don't see anything wrong or anything to be ashamed of in trying to show people that for once, the Rwandan government is serious in punishing people who commit those kinds of crimes."[22]

Major international human rights organisations appealed to President Pasteur Bizimungu again at the last minute to stop the executions. UN Human Rights Commissioner Mary Robinson said the executions did not meet internationally accepted standards "in which all guarantees of due process are strictly observed."[23] Mazimhaka responded by saying that the death penalty had been carried out in Rwanda for a century, first by the Belgian colonial authorities, then by the Hutu majority government for crimes "that pale in comparison (to genocide). I didn't hear the Pope ask for forgiveness then."[24]

Survivors of the 1994 genocide waited to watch the killers executed. Almost all of them lost relatives and friends in the pogroms.

The executions were carried out as scheduled in one of the most bizarre scenes ever witnessed in the embattled nation, as onlookers applauded the killings. A nation that had just suffered state-sanctioned terror which led to an unprecedented holocaust – in Rwandan history – four years earlier was now going through the same ritual of state-sponsored murder, but this time as a catharsis, and as an exercise in justice to exact retribution for the 1994 atrocities.

The executions were carried out in a theatrical ambiance reminiscent of Roman times.

It was carnival time. The people couldn't wait to enjoy themselves. The crowds were huge, with people whooping and clapping.[25] But that was only a part of this gory scene. It reminded one of the Roman era and its amphitheatres, especially the colosseum noted for its gladiatorial and wild beast displays up to the fifth century. According to a report from Rwanda:

"Before huge crowds of whooping, clapping Rwandans, 22 people convicted of organizing and leading this central African country's 1994 genocide were executed yesterday (April 24th) by firing squad....

In Kigali, the capital, an audience of 7,000 to 10,000 gathered to watch the execution of four of the prisoners, dressed in pale pink uniforms....

At 10:48 a.m., four masked police officers leaped from a truck and sprinted to within feet of the criminals, who each had a black square target on his chest. As bullets from

AK-47s shredded the prisoners' bodies, a sudden sharp silence descended on the crowd. Then a fifth marksman shot each prisoner in the head at point blank range. Twice. One onlooker sprinted and danced when the shooting stopped. Women ululated. A man named Andrew, 45, clapped lustly. 'God is great!' he cried."[26]

When the crowd erupted in cheers, celebrating the executions, another chapter in Rwandan history was being written. It was a chapter not only on justice but also on retribution.

And in spite of the gruesome nature of the executions, there was an unusual relaxed feeling even among the executioners themselves as if they were at a picnic. Executions carried out in other parts of the country were not much different from those which took place in the nation's capital Kigali. The executioners were just as relaxed: "In Nyamata, 30 miles south of Kigali, members of the firing squad reportedly replaced the clips of their AK-47s, as they took at least four minutes to kill the five condemned criminals there."[27]

When the Rwandan government announced the executions on April 22nd, it encouraged members of the public to attend and got an overwhelming response. Most of the people who attended the executions were Tutsis, of course, and they did so out of malicious vindictiveness probably more than anything else, although justice was also served. But that was not the only thing they wanted. The cheers and clapping during the executions clearly showed the people sought vengeance, more than justice, and were being highly vindictive.

Human rights groups condemned the executions for many reasons. The judges were not qualified and had only a few days of training in the rudimentaries of Rwandan law. Some of them were survivors of the genocide and were therefore automatically biased. Most of the defendants had no lawyers and were not allowed to cross-examine the prosecution's witnesses or present theirs; they had been tortured while in custody; they were tried on short notice and did not have enough time to prepare for the trials. And the proceedings were unusually short, in many cases lasting only a few hours, giving the defendants no time to respond to the charges.

It was kangaroo justice at its best. And it stampeded the accused through the courts all the way to the execution grounds.

Even some young Rwandans said the trials were deeply flawed. As Christine Mukaramongi, 19, said: "Those who planned genocide, they should be punished, but not executed. They should find another punishment...maybe jail for life."[28] But Rwandan officials were not impressed by that. They not only ignored such pleas and criticism before and after the executions but lashed out at foreign governments which claimed the moral high ground when they severely criticised the Rwandan government for executing the convicts.

And Rwanda officials seemed to have a valid point. They reminded foreign critics that had they responded quickly, they could have averted the catastrophe which claimed almost one million lives. As Kato Ninyetegeka, director of political affairs in the president's office, bluntly stated after watching the executions in the capital: "The international community has no moral authority to criticize the Rwandan government." He went on to say that the message Rwandans would get from the executions, the first in the country since 1982, was: "If I commit a crime, I will be punished – whether I am from the north or the south, or short or tall."[29]

The problem was that the majority of the Hutu, preoccupied with what they perceived to be the Tutsi menace and scourge, did not share that view. They saw themselves as victims of injustice under a judicial system, and a government, dominated by Tutsis; and in a country dominated by Tutsis practically in all walks of life. And the fact that probably most of the people who attended the executions were Tutsi only seemed to confirm that; so did the carnival atmosphere:

"An hour and 15 minutes before the scheduled time of execution, thousands in Kigali, including teenagers and children, snaked toward the red-earth soccer field, which is framed by lush green trees on surrounding hills. Thousands of others already rimmed the site, some perched in trees. The audience included hundreds of teenagers and children.

An excited, almost festive, mood prevailed among the spectators, who appeared to be mostly Tutsi. The crowd surged; police drove it back. When authorities arrived with the prisoners, the audience clapped. When the condemned were lashed by rope to nine-foot wooden posts, about six feet apart, the audience cheered.

Froduald Karamira, a former businessman and politician [who was a Tutsi and vice president of the extremist MDR-Power party under the former Hutu-dominated government of Juvénal Habyarimana – Karamira also formulated the concept of Hutu Power], received especially impassioned jeers. 'Karamira bye,' one woman shouted as the prisoners arrived. She waved across the field at Karamira, then cradled her young son's shoulders....

The three others (were) Virginie Mukankusi; Elie Nshimiyumeremyi, a Burundian who was a ringleader of Hutu killing squads here; and Silas Munyagishari, a former assistant prosecutor in Kigali.

Karamira, believed to be in his early 50s, controlled two of Rwanda's major radio stations during the genocide. One, the notorious Radio Mille Collines, broadcast hate propaganda against the Tutsi. He oversaw the vast network of roadblocks at which Hutu militiamen shot and hacked to death thousands of Tutsi in and around Kigali. 'During the genocide, Karamira was the star,' said Josue Kayijaho, chairman of a human rights organization and a leader of a genocide survivors' group. 'If he had said...'Stop the genocide,' a lot of people under his control would have stopped.'

Joyce Kayitesi, like many others, did not clap or cheer. She wept. Kayitesi, clutching a small package of white tissues, said Karamira had directed killers to her family during the genocide. Six of her relatives were slain. 'I felt upset, but I was also happy,' said Kayitesi, 21. 'It was a privilege [for those executed] to die like that. They killed us with hoes.'"[30]

The executions had immediate impact. It led to a flood of confessions from genocide suspects hoping to avoid the death penalty. And as one government official said after the first executions: "This is an ongoing process. They might resume next week, whether in public or in secret places depending on the lesson to be given."[31]

A senior official in the prosecutor's office in Kigali confirmed that the executions produced many confessions from jailed suspects: "Since...these executions, we have registered many applications for confession."[32] The executions on the outskirts of the capital, where the three men and a woman were shot by five policemen, were attended by a huge crowd of about 30,000 people.

Shortly after the executions, one of the most-wanted suspects in the 1994 genocide was arrested on orders of the UN International Criminal Tribunal for Rwanda (UNICTR) based in Arusha in neighbouring Tanzania. Colonel Alphonse Nteziryayo was captured on 28 April 1998 in Burkina Faso where he had sought refuge. He was accused of ordering Hutu extremists to kill all Tutsis in his jurisdiction.[33]

But whatever the outcome of his trial, it was clear that he would not get the death penalty. The war crimes tribunal did not have the mandate to impose a death sentence. The maximum sentence it could impose was life imprisonment.

That was one of the main reasons the Rwandan government did not want the genocide suspects to be tried by the war crimes tribunal in Tanzania. Rwandan leaders wanted the death penalty for many of the convicts, especially those who were the ringleaders during the genocide. And it was only in Rwandan courts where the death sentence could be imposed on them.

Although the executions scared many Hutu suspects into confessing their crimes committed during the genocide, they also inflamed passions among the Hutu and made reconciliation between the two ethnic groups even more difficult.

There was also a strong possibility that some of the accused accepted responsibility even for crimes they did not commit just to avoid the death penalty in Rwanda's notoriously biased kangaroo courts.

Therefore, justice was not served in all cases, and Rwanda remained a deeply divided country.

Misery and Conflict:
A Vicious Cycle

One of the unintended and most tragic consequences of the Rwandan conflict was the phenomenal increase in the number of AIDS cases across the country.

The epidemic spread like wild fire during the civil war, and Rwanda became an embattled nation in more than one way.

The country had just suffered a devastating blow during the genocide in 1994. The insurgency by Hutu rebels continued to claim more lives and disrupt society. The small, impoverished and overpopulated nation was inundated by a wave of returning refugees who put a severe strain on the country's meagre resources and aggravated communal conflict. And AIDS was wreaking havoc across that troubled land, reaching unprecedented levels during the same period when the poverty-stricken nation was unable to cope with this monumental crisis and other horrendous tragedies:

"Fanned by a decade of ethnic war and upheaval, a fast-growing AIDS epidemic has broken out of this country's cities and is sweeping through the rural areas, health officials and aid workers say.
Even if it is arrested now, the epidemic will take the life of one person out of 10 in the coming decade."[34]

That means, in a country of about 8 million people, at least 800,000 Rwandans will die of AIDS between 1998 and 2008, almost equal to the number of those who perished in the 1994 holocaust. And because the death toll from the AIDS epidemic has gone up dramatically in all African countries within only a few years, and estimates of the number of victims are usually lower than the actual number of cases, probably no fewer than 1 million Rwandans will die of AIDS within 10 years by 2008; a dreadful prospect.

A survey released in May 1998 showed that Rwanda's AIDS epidemic was one of the worst in Africa. At least 11% of Rwandans were HIV-positive, infected with the virus that causes AIDS, up from 1.3% in 1986.[35] The dramatic increase in AIDS was mostly attributed to the civil war and the mass movement of refugees from the conflict in the last four years since 1994. The upheaval loosened social structures and taboos against promiscuity, and perennial violence made it harder to persuade people not to engage in reckless sex, let alone scare them about a disease that may take years to claim its victims.

As the 2 million Hutu refugees fled from the victorious Tutsis who stopped the genocide, they spread AIDS among themselves and others, as did Hutu extremists and members of the Hutu national army who spearheaded the genocidal campaign. Rape, especially of Tutsi women, was common during the holocaust and as these murderers fled across the country in their way to refugee camps in Zaire and Tanzania. The camps themselves became hotbeds of prostitution, rape, and sexual promiscuity.

The continuing civil war in Rwanda also played a critical role in aggravating the situation. It helped to spread AIDS because of lack of security which kept health workers out of dangerous remote areas and hampered efforts to prevent AIDS. As Pascale Crussard, a nurse who directed the relief organisation CARE's anti-AIDS programme in Gitarama, central Rwanda, explained: "It's security. When people can die tomorrow from a machete wound, I'm not sure they think much about AIDS, from which they could die in 10 years."[36]

So, the attitude of many people was sex now or death from a machete blow.

The massacres also contributed substantially to the phenomenal rate of the pandemic, spreading to all parts of the country. Many people lost husbands and wives, boyfriends and girlfriends, during the genocide. The search for new partners and the desire to start new families was, unfortunately, fraught with danger. It was a minefield of AIDS, as sexual promiscuity became widespread during the search for companionship.

Culture was also a prime factor in the spread of the disease. The role culture played in spreading AIDS and other sex-related diseases showed that culture is indeed destiny. Like most Africans, Rwandans put a premium on having large families. Therefore, many women who lost their husbands during the genocide and ongoing conflict chose to have children out of wedlock and even shared a single male sexual partner who was not attached to any of them.

Also for cultural reasons, safe sex is unacceptable. Many Africans don't believe in using condoms to protect themselves. As some of them have explained, you can not eat candy with its wrapper on it.

Another cultural factor besides the importance of having many children which contributed to the high incidence of AIDS is polygamy whose matrimonial bonds entail sharing one husband. Just like any other people, many of them – husbands or wives in these polygamous families – are not faithful to their spouses, as the contraction of AIDS by these multiple sexual partners clearly shows. And they have played a major role in spreading the disease not only among themselves but to others.

Polygamy is very much an integral part of the institutional fabric that holds African societies together, sustaining traditional values including the imperative need to have large families, a point underscored by Eulerie Mukarugambwa, a mother of five whose husband was killed in the 1994 genocide, when she said: "We think about AIDS only afterwards, after the sexual act. There are women here who have lost children in the war and they just want to replace them."[37]

As AIDS continued to devastate the country, so did the war. The impact of the ethnic conflict – because of politicised ethnicity more than anything else – extended beyond the Rwandan borders and even claimed the lives of some Rwandans living in neighbouring countries after the massacre of Hutus in eastern Congo by Tutsi soldiers with the help of their fellow tribesmen, the Banyamulenge (Congolese Tutsis), who also live in that part of Congo.

One such victim was Seth Sendashonga. Sendashonga, 47, was Rwanda's interior minister from July 1994 until August 1995 when he was forced out of the Tutsi-dominated coalition government. He was shot dead in Nairobi, Kenya, on 16 May 1998 along with his Rwandan driver. After his expulsion from the government, he became a prominent opposition leader.

Rwanda's Foreign Minister Anastase Gasana denied on May 18th that Rwanda was behind the assassination: "We had a different political opinion, but Sendashonga was not a problem for the Rwandan government."[38]

Yet, as a prominent Hutu opposition leader and former cabinet member who held a senior post in the coalition government, it is highly probable that the Tutsi-dominated regime engineered Sendashonga's assassination despite Gasana's denials. And many Hutus were convinced that the Tutsi clique in Kigali masterminded what they saw as the political murder of one of the most prominent Hutu leaders opposed to Tutsi domination of Rwanda.

Hutu opposition to Tutsi domination continued to take a violent form when Hutu rebels killed hundreds of civilians in northwestern Rwanda towards the end of May 1998. It was one of the deadliest attacks since the end of the 1994 genocide:

"Machete-wielding Hutu rebels attacked hundreds of civilians in northwestern Rwanda, apparently to punish them for seeking protection from the Tutsi-led army, a UN official said yesterday (May 28th). As many as 1,000 may have been killed, the official said."[39]

A reviled institution among the Hutu, the Tutsi-dominated army was an embodiment of all that was wrong with Rwanda: Tutsi oppression and exploitation of the Hutu, and persecution and indiscriminate killings of Hutu civilians. And any Hutu who sought protection from the the army was considered to be a traitor and became fair game for the rebels. In fact, he was seen not only as a traitor; he was no better than and was sometimes even worse than the villains who were protecting him and undermining the struggle for Hutu liberation from brutal subjugation by the Tutsi.

The attacks were brutal, with many survivors mutilated, and the standard weapon being the machete:

"They included a 3-year-old girl whose arm had been

chopped off and a 4-year-old boy whose leg had been cut off below the knee....

The victims blamed the rebels for a series of attacks that began Sunday (May 23rd)."[40]

The attacks took place in Mutura and Rwerere districts on the foothills of the volcanic Virunga Mountains where the rebels were hiding. The mountains are close to the Rwandan-Congolese border. The attacks were aimed at punishing the estimated 15,000 civilians, most of them Hutu, who had fled their villages since March 1998 because of the guerrilla insurgency but returned to their homes under the protection of the Tutsi-dominated Rwandan Patriotic Army (RPA).

The rebels were further inflamed when one of the most prominent leaders of the 1994 genocide was sentenced to death around the same time. According to *The Economist*:

"Professor Geoffrey Gatera, former head of Rwanda's university medical school, was sentenced to death by a court in Butare for his involvement in the massacre of hundreds of Tutsis in 1994 who had sought refuge in the hospital."[41]

He was the first prominent academic to receive the death sentence in the genocide trials. His sentencing came in the midst of an escalating, brutal civil conflict in which countless civilians were killed after the 1994 genocide: "Many of the former Hutu government soldiers and militiamen responsible for carrying out the genocide of minority Tutsi and politically moderate Hutu...returned to Rwanda in November (and December) 1996. Since then, thousands of people – Hutu and Tutsi – have died in rebel attacks on schools, bars, buses and homes."[42]

The murders were committed by both sides. Reprisals by the army, in retaliation for rebel attacks, led to indiscriminate killings of Hutus, thus exacerbating ethnic tensions in a country where relations between the two ethnic groups were already polarised even though attempts were being made by different organisations to achieve reconciliation.

In another deadly attack, Hutu rebels killed 34 people in a village bar as they watched the World Cup final soccer match in mid-July 1998.[43] Around the same time, a Rwandan court in the capital Kigali convicted four persons on charges of genocide. Two of them were sentenced to death. Mrs. Euphrasie Kamatamu, 54, a former councilor, was convicted of organising the massacre of Tutsis and politically moderate Hutus in Kigali in 1994. Mrs. Kamatamu and her husband were sentenced to death on 17 July 1998 after being found guilty of drawing up death lists, distributing weapons to Hutu militiamen and manning roadblocks to stop Tutsis from escaping the genocide. The other two received life sentences.[44]

Rwanda's cycle of misery and conflict also included kidnappings. On 21 July 1998, Hutu rebels kidnapped two Belgian missionaries in northern Rwanda. The missionaries, Reverend Mark Francois and Reverend Jean Lefevre, were abducted by a group of 150 armed Hutu insurgents.[45]

The motive behind many of the kidnappings in the Rwandan civil war, like similar abductions in conflicts in other African countries including neighbouring Congo and Burundi, included extortion and publicity for the rebel cause.

The rebels continued to pursue their cause violently. On 31 July 1998, they hacked to death at least 110 people in the communes of Buheta and Raba about 30 miles northwest of Kigali. As in most attacks, the rebels were armed with machetes imported from the People's Republic of China, and clubs. Fred Ibingira, the military commander responsible for Kigali and the Kigali rural prefecture of Rushishi which included the communes of Buheta and

Raba, said the attackers included residents from the area. They also burned down a local official's house.[46]

The attack was the worst since the rebels killed 34 people in mid-July at a roadside inn on the main road between Kigali and the northwestern region.

In spite of attempts by the government to isolate the rebels, the insurgents continued to rely on their fellow tribesmen for food, shelter and money; the kind of ethnic solidarity which could sustain the guerrilla campaign indefinitely unless the demands of the Hutu majority for justice and equality were fully addressed by the Tutsi-dominated government.

It was a regime which had no mandate to rule because it was founded on the premise of inequality. Many Tutsis, as a product of "superior stock," felt that they had the right to be on top, a superstition that was invoked to justify the politics of exclusion at the expense of the Hutu majority.

The turmoil in Rwanda took another turn in September 1998 when the rebels launched a daring raid which led to what was probably the biggest jail break in the country's history. The offensive was directly related to the trial and convictions of Hutu leaders by the international criminal tribunal in neighbouring Tanzania for their role in orchestrating and masterminding the 1994 genocide in which more than 75% of the Tutsi population of Rwanda – 1 in every 10 Rwandans – was wiped out; an average of 8,000 killings per day.

The insurgents "stormed a prison in western Rwanda and freed 3,000 inmates suspected of involvement in the 1994 genocide....However, most of the inmates returned voluntarily to the prison, afraid of army reprisals if they are associated with the rebels, said Rwandan officials who spoke on condition of anonymity. A group of rebels overpowered guards and set inmates free Friday (September 4th) at Kivumu prison about 60 miles west of the capital, Kigali....The breakout occurred after two former senior Rwandan officials were convicted of war crimes last week in Tanzania."[47]

Prisons and jails were some of the biggest targets for the rebels during the post-genocide period in order to free their kinsmen, about 130,00 of whom were confined awaiting trial, and to show that they were important players on the Rwandan political scene – and must be taken into account in any attempt to resolve the conflict. Exclude them, forget peace. Ignore them at your peril.

In what amounted to a partial victory for the Hutu, the Rwandan government announced in October 1998 that it would free 10,000 suspects held in jails and prisons across the country awaiting trial for genocide. Justice Minister Faustin Ntezilyayo said their files contained no concrete evidence against them,[48] a rare concession by the government.

And it was the right decision, especially when a number of factors which had direct bearing on the dispensation of justice in the post-genocide period are taken into account: Rwanda's legal system was shattered after four years of civil conflict; most of the judges and court officials had either fled or had been killed; and the people who replaced them, most of them Tutsis in a vengeful mood, had not received adequate legal training to administer justice accordingly.

There was also strong international pressure on Rwanda to alleviate the plight of the tens of thousands of Hutus confined in filthy, overcrowded prisons where they were packed into small cells like sardines in a can, with no indication when they would be tried, if at all.

After the predominantly Tutsi Rwandan Patriotic Front (RPF) seized power in July 1994, many Hutus were detained for nothing. They were arrested simply because someone, usually a Tutsi, pointed a finger at them without any credible evidence against the accused; or simply because they were Hutu and therefore automatically suspected of having participated in the massacre of Tutsis.

The justice minister said the detainees whose files contained only personal information such as their names and birth dates but no concrete evidence against them would be released. However, the decision did not have any dampening effect on the insurgency in different parts of the country, especially in the northwest where the rebels were waging a vicious campaign against civilians and the army.

The insurgency was only a part of the larger regional problem posing a threat to the security and survival of the Tutsi in Congo, Rwanda, and Burundi. As Rwanda's Vice President and Defence Minister Paul Kagame said in an interview with *The Christian Science Monitor*:

"The issue is always: If somebody doesn't ensure your security and instead causes insecurity to you, what do you do? My job is to deal with that eventuality. But I certainly would be a very, very happy person if I didn't have to deal with these uncertainties....

Initially, we had hoped to handle (the problem of Hutu extremists hiding in Congo) adequately with (Laurent) Kabila's government. Apparently, the decision has turned out to be the opposite effect."[49]

Hutu rebels wreaking havoc in northwestern Rwanda and other parts of the country, especially in areas close to the Rwandan-Congolese border, launched some of their deadliest attacks from their operational bases in eastern Congo, forcing the Rwandan leadership to contend with a double threat to the nation's security: attacks from within and from across the border. It was this threat which prompted the Rwandan government to publicly execute 22 people convicted of genocide as a warning to the insurgents.

The executions were also intended to punish the guilty. And that may indeed have been the immediate objective. They were also aimed at extracting confessions from other suspects languishing in prison under appalling conditions. But the overriding concern was long-term security for the Tutsi minority. It was in pursuit of this long-term objective that Rwandan officials felt they could defy international opinion against the executions without fear of sanctions.

And the executions did frighten many suspects into confessing when they otherwise would not have. Such swift retribution, perceived as an injustice by many Hutus and critics of Rwanda's judicial system, also led to more convictions:

"In the capital city of Kigali and the regions of Gikongoro, Nyamata, Murambi, and Kibungo, 22 Hutus convicted of genocide and the mass murder of Tutsis and moderate Hutus in 1994 (were) publicly executed by firing squad (on 24 April 1998). Rwanda's Tutsi-controlled government, acting independently of the International Criminal Tribunal for Rwanda, ignored appeals from the US, the EU (European Union), and several human rights organizations to stay the executions on the grounds that the convicts' trial failed to meet international standards of justice.

The Justice Ministry announce(d) (on) May 15 that at Kirima prison, south of Kigali, some 2,000 Rwandans accused of participating in the 1994 genocide have written statements admitting their involvement in order to avoid execution. Under Rwandan law, defendants who confess are eligible for reduced sentences, in this case life in prison instead of execution....

(On) May 28 UN officials report(ed) that 3 days ago in northwestern Rwanda, Hutu rebels killed 94 civilians and wounded 67 because they had sought protection of the country's Tutsi-led army.

The government has recently begun a campaign to persuade Hutus in the northwest to deny food, shelter, and money to the rebels.

(On) June 2 a Rwandan court sentence(d) to death 5

Hutu rebels for killing 4 UN human rights monitors in February 1997.

(On) June 6 Rwandan radio report(ed) that a court in the northeastern town of Byumba ha(d) convicted 38 people of genocide in the 1994 killings, sentencing 35 to life in prison and 3 to lesser sentences....

(On) August 4 government forces kill(ed) 60 Hutu rebels in the town of Rusebeya in northwestern Rwanda."[50]

That was only part of the picture of Rwanda in her years of turmoil. And it remained a permanent fixture on the political landscape of this deeply troubled nation for many years, as many people in and outside Rwanda sought ways to end the perennial conflict between the Hutu and the Tutsi. Tragically, the biggest players in this tragic drama – the government and the rebels – chose violence as the best solution to the problem. But violence was a two-edged sword. It cut both ways.

Although the rebels inflicted heavy casualties on the civilian population as part of their broader strategy to destabilise the country and undermine the government, they also sustained heavy losses, now and then, at the hands of the Tutsi-dominated army. One of the biggest blows they suffered was in October 1998 when the army killed 378 of them in the northwestern region.[51] But the insurgents were able to absorb the loss because of the support they had among their fellow tribesmen, the Hutu majority. The attack also helped the insurgents to recruit even more fighters.

Hutu ethnonationalism – call it raw-naked tribalism or whatever you want to call it – played a critical role in the campaign. Many young Hutus felt that it was their patriotic duty to join the rebel forces fighting for the rights of the Hutu majority who constituted the Hutu nation, a nation that was being brutally subjugated by "alien invaders from Ethiopia," the Tutsi.

As long as the Tutsi were perceived to be outsiders, the Hutu population – the majority of whom also shared this false perception contrived by the Hutu elite for political purposes – would continue to be fertile ground for recruitment of more and more guerrilla fighters, thus perpetuating the conflict; a conflict that was also perpetuated by the Tutsi rulers who refused to concede the legitimacy of the Hutu's demands for equality and justice on the basis of a pluralistic consensus.

One of the most brutal policies pursued by the predominantly Tutsi government to control and subjugate the Hutu majority was *imudugudusization*, forcing people to live in "protected" villages. Vietnam, Rhodesia, and Ethiopia under Mengistu Haile Mariam, among other countries, tried it before. Burundi also tried enforced villagisation, with tragic consequences.

But it only caused immense suffering among the peasants, most of them desperately poor, and it failed. The governments which pursued this policy – in Africa and in Asia – lost the war against the insurgents and alienated the vast majority of their people.

Yet Rwanda never learned a lesson from any of that and proceeded to institute its own "concentration camps." As reported by *The Economist*:

"It is not setting up strategic hamlets with barbed wire but it is proposing a controversial programme that is designed to transform Rwanda's troubled north-west province for the better, but seems likely to create more problems than it solves....

The people to be put in the villages are mainly Hutu peasants, a group still uncertain of their place in the new Rwanda and not entirely trusted by the Tutsi-led government....

Under the new scheme, scattered dwellings and hillside plots are discouraged, and people are urged to live together at new sites close to the roads. Here, the government says, they will eventually form *imudugudus*, special villages with shared services like water, clinics and schools. A cooperative farming system will be set up, and they will be offered a range of activities to earn some cash. And, of course, being near the road, they will be safer, close to military patrols.

Villagisation has already been attempted in other parts of Rwanda, notably at Kibungo in the south-east, where big housing projects were created for returning Hutu refugees. But the north-west was, until recently, a war zone. In the past two years, remnants of the Interahamwe militias, the Hutu groups responsible for much of the 1994 genocide, have raided villages, attacked minibus taxis and killed local officials, all in the name of 'liberating Hutus from Tutsi domination.' Their campaign has been helped by their ability to blend in with ordinary villagers, using traditional loyalties or brute force to get support and assistance. They have been adept at using the mountainous terrain."[53]

The collectivisation programme was similar to the establishment of *ujamaa* villages in neighbouring Tanzania but for different reasons. While the programme in Tanzania focused on economic development and improvement in the provision of social services, the villagisation policy pursued by the Tutsi-dominated Rwandan government was driven by security concerns to isolate Hutu rebels from the civilian population – their Hutu kinsmen – they used as a cover to carry out their activities, mostly attacks on civilian and government targets in different parts of the country.

Counter-insurgency operations against the rebels led to indiscriminate killings of Hutu civilians, atrocities the government tried to justify by contending that it was impossible to distinguish the rebels from civilians. Therefore the killing of Hutu civilians was no more than collateral damage that is expected in any war.

41

The government's scorched-earth policy included deliberate destruction of banana plants and entire villages, ostensibly to deprive the insurgents of cover for their operations. But it was a policy that was really intended to starve Hutus into submission, as the deliberate destruction of their villages and crops, especially bananas which is their staple food, clearly showed. And it alienated Hutu peasants, the very same people the government claimed it was trying to protect, and with their approval.

Like all governments which set up strategic hamlets or moved people to "protected" areas away from the combat zone, the Rwandan regime falsely claimed that Hutu peasants wanted to be relocated in those villages. Some of them sought protection from the army. But that was not true in most cases:

"Hundreds of thousands of Hutus have fled their homes and been gathered into a dozen temporary camps. Officially, this was called a 'voluntary migration.' In fact, there was not much voluntary about it, as the army swept across the hills, forcing Hutus into the valleys below."[54]

They fled their homes because of the war, running away from Tutsi soldiers. More than anything else, it was the army's brutal and indiscriminate counter-insurgency operations – directed against the Hutu civilian population, and not specifically against the insurgents – which forced them to flee.

But it is equally true that both sides used terror to achieve their goals. A lot of times, Hutu rebels terrorised and killed their own people, fellow Hutus, especially if they did not support them. The government tried to capitalise on that.

Rwandan leaders justified the relocation of the Hutu civilian population as a compassionate policy intended to protect them. But there was nothing compassionate about it. Enforce villagisation did not alleviate their plight and

42

had none of the redeeming qualities claimed by its exponents, the Tutsi rulers.

In October 1998, the United Nations denounced the policy and warned of a potential human catastrophe in the "protected" villages where people lived in horrible conditions, making them highly vulnerable to disease. Enforced villagisation, which was tantamount to internment, was opposed not only by Hutu peasants but also by some local officials and church leaders.

It was a policy imposed from above without any input from the people it was supposedly intended to help. As one diplomat in Kigali said:

"I have talked to farmers, local officials, even some ministers, and all think this is a bad idea. They talk about having consulted everyone, but it's another case of the top-down approach: we think for them."[55]

And it had tragic consequences for the country. Enforced villagisation – which included destruction of crops and traditional Hutu villages by the Tutsi-dominated army – not only alienated the Hutu majority; it fuelled the insurgency, thus achieving exactly the opposite of what the government had hoped to achieve. It also encouraged many young Hutus to join the rebellion and won the rebels more support from their tribesmen in the rural areas, the primary target of this brutal policy of *imudugudusization*, because many of them saw the rebels as freedom fighters, fighting for the rights of the Hutu majority.

Attempts to placate the Hutu majority failed, mainly because the government was not genuine in its commitment to the egalitarian ideals it espoused. The Hutu felt they had been left out even out of representation at the local level.

At the end of March 1999, Rwandans elected 116,000 officials in the country's 154 communes. But none of the candidates represented any political party, a decision that came from the top. And there was no electoral campaign. Yet government officials hailed the exercise as "participatory democracy" at the grassroots level."[56]

The Tutsi-dominated government maintained a tight grip on the Hutu majority and never intended to allow much democracy in the country. According to a report on the controlled elections – conducted from 29 to 31 March – in *The Economist*:

"These were very much local elections, in which groups of 50 – 100 families chose ten-member committees to administer their affairs. The committees will, in turn, vote for officials to run larger areas, of up to 5,000 people. There were no parties, no balloting, no polling booths....That seems to be as much democracy as the Rwandan Patriotic Front (RPF) government will allow for the moment....

Though Tutsis account for only a small proportion of Rwanda's population, the most powerful people in the government are all Tutsi. They are unwilling to sanction full democracy."[57]

If democracy is not applied to national leaders, enabling the people to vote for them, then they don't have the mandate to rule. It is inequity of power that rankles the powerless Hutu majority. And it will continue to fuel ethnic conflict indefinitely.

The quest for national unity through centralisation of power at the national level is no more than an ethnic enterprise by the politically dominant Tutsis to perpetuate themselves in office by suffocating dissent among the Hutu majority.

Yet the Tutsi also have legitimate fear of exclusion from power and even extermination should their adversaries prevail in a genuine democratic contest, as they are bound to, given their numerical superiority:

"Some Rwandans see the RPF's attempt to promote national unity through limited democracy as a cynical ploy (by the Tutsi) to maintain power. But the truth is that the government knows that democracy would be political suicide, and possibly not just political.

It is urgently seeking a formula that would be reasonably democratic and, at the same time, protect the Tutsi minority."[58]

The question is how the Tutsi minority can be protected in a country ruled by the Hutu majority – as it definitely would be, perpetually, without the Hutu losing any election to the Tutsi minority – and how Hutus can be protected from the politically dominant Tutsis who have no intention of relinquishing control or introducing true democracy because they are afraid they will be exterminated if they are forced out of power democratically or militarily.

It is a puzzle which has led some African leaders – not just Kenyan President Daniel arap Moi – to conclude that separation of the two ethnic groups through partition of both Rwanda and Burundi is the only solution left after everything else that has been tried has failed to solve the problem.

It is also a dilemma the Tutsi-dominated government failed to resolve precisely because it refused to make significant concessions to the Hutu majority. It could have done that through devolution of power to the regions – prefectures – and all the way down to the grassroots level. Without such compromise, it is difficult to see how Rwanda, or any other African country, can continue to exist as a stable and united political entity.

Even Rwandans themselves ask the same question about their country, as they indeed should more than anybody else. As *The New York Times* in its edition of 6 April 1999 stated in a report from Rwanda on the fifth anniversary of the 1994 genocide aptly headlined "Hutu and Tutsi Ask: Is a Unified Rwanda Possible?":

"Salviana Mukagatare, 30, (is a Tutsi)....A triangular scar – three chops from a machete – runs from below her right eye to her ear. Her right hand, chopped twice, is a limp claw. She is the only member of her family to survive the massacres in her village in April 1994. 'Forgive?' she asked. 'No, I can't'....

Hutu and Tutsi are living side by side, as they did for centuries....Yet hope sits alongside a fair share of pessimism. Many say Hutu and Tutsi are still far apart in their hearts. Intermarriage, once so common it is hard to tell who is who, is now rare....

And the Government...faces criticism from growing corruption and...uneven distribution of property and jobs.

In an interview last week, Major-General Paul Kagame, who led the army of exiled Tutsi who took power in 1994, admitted to some of the worst of the accusations, including reports that his soldiers had killed civilians in their fights against Hutu extremists. But overall, he contended, the Government has done its best to root out excesses and recreate Rwanda. 'After five years, there is a long way to go,' said Mr. Kagame, 41, the Vice President and the nation's real political power. 'We can't overcome this complex situation in five years.'"[59]

He was right. It was going to take more than five years to rebuild Rwanda and to reconcile the two ethnic groups, if they could be reconciled at all. But that did not explain the continued indiscriminate killings and systematic torture of countless Hutu civilians or the the exclusion of the Hutu majority from power; nor did it explain or justify the pattern of systematic discrimination against Hutus in employment, education and other areas.

The government did very little to correct those injustices after the Tutsi seized power and stopped the genocide in 1994. And the holocaust continued to have an impact on the lives of most Rwandans in the post-genocide period:

"Some critics wonder how long the Government can keep its mandate, which rests on its having defeated the Hutu powers that planned and carried out the killings. But there is no question that the events that began on April 6, 1994 – when the plane of the Hutu President, Juvénal Habyarimana, was shot down and the organized massacre of the Tutsi erupted – still seep into every corner of life."[60]

One can understand why the Tutsi would not want to relinquish power to the people who almost wiped them out, especially only a few years after the genocide, and even after 100 years. The memories of the 1994 holocaust and its aftermath were still fresh in their minds and would probably remain so for the rest of their lives, unlike their adversaries, the Hutu, who were never – and who, because of their numerical superiority, could never be – threatened with annihilation by the Tutsi.

Yet, even such pragmatic considerations could not be used to justify denying the Hutu their rights including their legitimate status as the nation's majority entitled to democratic rule; nor did the Tutsi regime have the right to neutralise their struggle for justice and equality in a pluralistic context. They had legitimate aspirations.

But the Tutsi also had legitimate fear for their security and wellbeing probably even more so than the Hutu because of their status as a distinct minority. They could, indeed, be annihilated if Hutu extremists came to power. Even five years after the genocide, the situation remained tense:

"By any measure, Rwanda remains a traumatized country. It has not even cleared all its human debris. Bits of leg bone, a child's sandal, poke out from the rubble in two rooms on the church grounds in Nyarabuye, where

10,000 were killed."[61]

And the skulls of many who died in a classroom where they sought shelter were still on display in memory of all those who perished in the holocaust and as a reminder of what happened during that horrendous tragedy. This was just one of the macabre memorial sites preserved across Rwanda. One of the most well-known massacres besides the one in Nyarabuye and elsewhere took place in Kibeho in southwestern Rwanda.

About 20,000 Tutsis were massacred at the Catholic Church in the town of Kibeho.[62] According to a report from Kibeho by *The New York Times*:

"The floor of the church is now covered with moss. The burned-out roof is open to the sky, and in a macabre memorial just down the hill, the corpses of people who died are now mummified, lying twisted on shelves, some with rosaries around their necks.

It was five years ago today (7 April) that thousands of Tutsi...gathered at the church here, afraid of bands of Hutu who had begun an attempt at genocide....Several thousand of them...died...here.

Today, leaders of Rwanda came here to give some of the dead a proper burial, in the biggest of several memorial services around the nation....

Kibeho was one of hundreds of places around the country where well-organized bands of Hutu militia attacked their Tutsi neighbors, mostly hacking them to death....Kibeho is also where, in April 1995, Tutsi-led Government troops cleared a huge refugee camp it claimed was full of Hutu extremists. Human rights officials say that at least 4,000 Hutu were killed, many shot and many trampled. There was no official mention of that incident today."[63]

It was such neglect and abuse of power by the Tutsi-

48

dominated government, and blatant discrimination as well as indiscriminate killings, which alienated that vast majority of Hutus from the nation's leadership despite its pledge to pursue reconciliation in that war-torn and ethnically divided country.

Hutu guerrillas were the biggest beneficiaries of this official neglect, and discrimination, which drove more and more young Hutus into their ranks. It also enabled the insurgents to win more sympathy from their fellow tribesmen for their cause, however reprehensible their tactics. Reconciliation of the two ethnic groups was impossible under those circumstances. And the least reconciliatory gesture by the government was, rightly or wrongly, automatically seen by many Hutus as an affront. They did not believe the regime really wanted to pursue reconciliation.

Yet, even in the midst of such polarisation, the country continued to seek reconciliation although it remained a distant goal which may never be fully realised, given the level of hostility and deep mistrust between the two groups. According to a report by Lora Santoro from Rwanda's capital, Kigali, in *The Christian Science Monitor.*

"Five years after the genocide, the scars are still fresh, and the problems of coexistence (between Hutus and Tutsis) at close quarters seemingly insurmountable....

(The) judicial system is dealing with more than 150,000 genocide suspects sitting in Rwanda's jails....

Given the magnitude of the genocide, reconciliation will take decades."[64]

It may indeed take decades, if at all. But prospects for such reconciliation are bleak at best.

Reconciliation entailed justice, which mostly included prosecuting the perpetrators of the 1994 genocide some of whom were clergymen. One of the highest church officials to be arrested was a Roman Catholic bishop, Augustin Misago, one week after the fifth anniversary of the holocaust: "Justice Minister Jean de Dieu Mucyo said the clergyman...was being held in 'preventive detention' until authorities decide whether to try him in Kigali, the capital, or in his diocese of Gikongoro in southern Rwanda."[65]

Rwandan President Pasteur Bizimungu, who as a Hutu was no more than a figurehead in the Tutsi-dominated government controlled by Vice President and Defence Minister Paul Kagame, said Bishop Misago refused to provide sanctuary to fleeing Tutsis who faced death at the hands of Hutu extremists in Gikongoro prefecture.[66]

The charge was backed up by Tutsi survivors of the massacres. As one genocide survivor, an old woman waiting outside the courtroom where Bishop Misago was being tried in the capital Kigali, said: "I lost my mother, my father, my sister, and all my brothers. He never helped anyone, even though he had the power to, he never lifted a finger. I know what he did."[67]

Misago was accused of turning over three Tutsi priests to Hutu killers, and of refusing to help 30 Tutsi school girls who were in danger of being killed by the militiamen. The girls were later killed. The bishop was also accused of sending to their deaths 16 schoolgirls whom he had expelled from Kibeho High School in the town of Kibeho, 60 miles southwest of Kigali, in his diocese. Bishop Misago was one of the country's 11 bishops arrested for genocide. According to *The New York Times*:

"Bishop Misago's arrest appeared imminent after President Bizimungu, speaking at the fifth anniversary of the killings at Kibeho..., called for the Bishop to explain himself publicly.

Bishop Misago, who was present at the ceremony that honored 20,000 Tutsi who were killed at the town's Catholic church, did not answer accusations against him....

African Rights, a human rights groups, made public a

report...calling for Pope John Paul II to aid the investigation into Bishop Misago's role in the killings.

Bishop Misago is the highest-ranking church official to be arrested on genocide charges. So far, 19 Rwandan priests have been jailed on suspicion of aiding the killings....More than 1,000 (genocide suspects) have been tried.

Relations between the Government and the Catholic church have been tense. Survivors groups have demanded a public apology from the Catholic clergy for the killings in churches and missionary-run schools, where thousands of Tutsi were hacked and burned to death by Hutu soldiers and militiamen, sometimes with the complicity of the priests."[68]

In a country that is predominantly Hutu, and whose Christian population is also mostly Hutu, such an apology was unlikely although appropriate. But even if it was given, it would have amounted to nothing. Even trials – by village elders and peers under a traditional system called *gacaca* – of some of the people who participated in the genocide, a proposal put forward by the government, drew strong criticism from the members of both ethnic groups.

Hutus feared that it would be a witch hunt. Tutsis worried that in communities that are predominantly Hutu, as most are in a country which is itself overwhelmingly Hutu, genocide suspects would not be found guilty, and they would not be punished, even if there was overwhelming evidence to convict them, showing that they participated in the genocide. As Aloys Habimana, director of the Rwandan League for the Promotion and Defence of Human Rights, stated:

"There is a kind of ethnic tension which is persistent in the population. And as far as they are unable to overcome this, it will be difficult for them to be fair."[69]

Even the country's Roman Catholic bishops expressed profound concern about genocide trials under this system, *gacaca* (pronounced *ga – Cha – cha*), and told Rwanda's prime minister that it "might become an instrument of injustice."[70]

The government proposed to use the traditional system because Rwanda's courts were overburdened by the genocide trials. But even the most ardent supporters of this approach urged caution because the trials would not be conducted by impartial panels for one simple reason: The people presiding over the trials would come from the very same communities where the crimes took place. Therefore dispensation of justice would be tainted by bias and compromised by conflict of interest.

Yet, many prisoners thought trial under *gacaca* was a good idea, for obvious reasons. As 54-year-old Azalyas Rukizangabo, who was accused of killing two women, said: "Once we go to the place we are born, people can say, this man has done nothing."[71] But as Abbey Alphonse Mazimpaka, a police prosecutor in Nyarubuye District, put it: "*Gacaca* is the reconciliation between the victim and the criminal. After negotiating, you reconcile. But how can a person negotiate with someone who did these acts of bloodshed and sexual torture? It is impossible."[72]

In traditional rural Rwanda, village elders mediate disputes. And they earn their position by virtue of seniority. Under a modified version of *gacaca* for genocide trials, the judges would be elected by members of the community.

Justice Minister Jean de Dieu Mucyo, a Tutsi genocide survivor, said *gacaca* was aimed not only at clearing the prisons but also at speeding reconciliation between the Hutu and the Tutsi. As he put it:

"Without the truth coming out, everyone is holding feelings inside and it's really oppressive to the heart. But if the truth can come out, everyone can know what happened: 'This one killed my brother,' or 'My son is in jail for this reason.' With the truth coming out, everyone will be relieved."73

This is similar to the Truth and Reconciliation Commission (TRC) in South Africa after the end of apartheid. But even there, no one is sure how much reconciliation really took place between whites and blacks as well as other non-whites who suffered under that diabolical institution.

In the case of Rwanda, the most serious cases – murder, planning murder, rape, all of which carried the death penalty – would be adjudicated in conventional courts. The justice minister said any member of the community would be allowed to testify, and that defendants would be given the opportunity to refute the charges. However, all the proceedings would be conducted without trained judges or lawyers; and the majority of the judges on the panel would decide whether the accused was guilty or innocent.

Yet many critics contended that without lawyers, the accused would not be able to represent themselves adequately. Others said *gacaca* had been a way for people in the rural areas to settle their own disputes, usually minor ones, before village elders. They questioned how this traditional approach could be taken in today's Rwanda where so many people were new to the country. About one million Tutsis, roughly equal to the number of their kinsmen who were massacred, returned to Rwanda after living an entire generation in exile in neighbouring countries.

A very large number of them, probably the majority, were not even born in Rwanda or left Rwanda when they were only babies or children, as was the case with Paul Kagame himself, the most powerful man in the country, who left his homeland with his parents for Uganda when he was a very small child, about three years old. They hardly knew anything about *gacaca*, if at all. They were more Ugandan, Burundian, Tanzanian and Congolese than Rwandan, and entirely so in terms of upbringing.

That alone was a major obstacle to reconciliation with the people – the Hutu – who had lived and grown up in Rwanda, in a different culture, all those years, during which they discriminated against the Tutsi who remained in the country and later committed some of the worst massacres in modern history. And the hostility between the members of the two groups was unmistakable even in neighbouring countries where they lived as refugees, especially after the 1994 genocide. As Roger Rosenblatt wrote in *The New Republic*:

"(In 1999) Tanzania contain(ed) over 230,000 Burundians and Congolese, as well as Rwandans.

Rwandans are currently spread out among 14 countries in Africa....

In 1994, at a camp in Tanzania, across the border from bloody Rwanda,...the Tutsis...lived side by side with their killers. I talked with both terrified Tutsi families and with Hutu young men who made no secret of their desire to finish the work they had begun in Rwanda."[74]

And it was no secret that, even with the defeat they had suffered many times in their clashes with the Tutsi-dominated army, they had not given up. And there were countless others, young and older Hutus, across Rwanda who harboured the same sentiment: wipe them out. The problem was how to induce them to abandon their genocidal mission, while they remained on the periphery of the political mainstream dominated by the very same people they wanted to exterminate.

While many Rwandans were debating the merits, and demerits, of the *gacaca* traditional judicial system, and questioning its ability to handle genocide trials, conventional courts and military tribunals continued to dispense justice in cases involving murder and other serious offences committed during the holocaust.

Some of those who were convicted were members of the clergy. In June 1999, "a pastor from Rwanda's Episcopal Church and a former army major were condemned to death for genocide by a special military tribunal....It was the first time that such a senior officer had been condemned by a Rwandan court for the mass killings in 1994."[75]

The two men were among the most prominent convicts to receive the death sentence in Rwanda.

Just the day before the two men were sentenced to death in Kigali, another "court...sentenced 9 people to death and 16 to life in prison on charges related to the country's 1994 genocide....The sentences were handed down in two separate trials in Kibuye, where four years ago Hutu soldiers, militiamen and civilians almost wiped out their Tutsi neighbors in 90 days of killings orchestrated by the former Hutu government."[76]

Had the trials taken place under the *gacaca* traditional system, presided over by judges – most likely Hutu – from the same community where the Hutu defendants came from, it is highly probable that the accused would not have been convicted. They would have been acquitted regardless of how much evidence was marshalled against them confirming their guilt.

As the trials continued in Rwanda's conventional courts, the Catholic Church came under scrutiny for its role in helping Hutu militias exterminate the Tutsi. After the arrest of Bishop Augustin Misago who was denied bail, other priests and nuns were arrested, suspected of complicity in the mass murder of Tutsis and moderate Hutus. According to *World Press*:

"Misago's arrest has put a spotlight on mounting evidence of involvement in the genocide by representatives of the Catholic church in Rwanda.

More than 30 priests, brothers, and nuns are being held in Rwanda for their role in the murders, and two priests have been sentenced to death, Baptiste Kayigamba (of Inter Press Service), writes.

According to a report in the Lyons-based Catholic monthly *Colias*, recounted by Daniel Licht in the *Libération* of Paris, the church was involved in an operation to whisk away and protect some 60 Rwandan priests of the White Fathers missionary order who are suspected of crimes in Rwanda.

'*Colias*'s investigators believe the church used an escape network that extended from Kigali via Rome and Paris to Belgian, French, and Italian dioceses,' Licht reports."[77]

Gerard Chabon, father superior of the White Fathers order in France, told Daniel Licht of the Paris-based *Liberation*: "All of these allegations are unfounded."[78]

But there was enough evidence against the 60 Hutu priests who were spirited out of Rwanda to bring them to trial for their involvement in the massacres of Tutsis in the 1994 genocide.

Their escape was a denial of justice to the survivors of the holocaust. It also somehow impeded the reconciliation process. Any exoneration of those accused of genocide, and attempts by them to circumvent the law, only inflamed passions among the Tutsi, the primary victims of the holocaust.

Even participatory justice under the traditional system of *gacaca* – a term used to describe a field of grass or an open space in which, under traditional law, members of a community gather to arbitrate small disputes – which could enable Tutsi victims to become judges, was not enough to convince them that the guilty would get the punishment they deserved.

And most Hutus felt that they were not even guilty of genocide, if one took place at all. It was simply a liberation war, a war for the survival of the Hutu nation, many of them argued, and must be looked at in that context. As Lora Santoro reported from Rwanda in *The Christian Science Monitor*:

"Behind the notion of participatory justice (under *gacaca*), adds Rwanda's justice minister, Jean de Dieu Mucyo, lies the deeper issue of reconciliation between Rwanda's Hutu population, an 85 percent majority, and the Tutsi minority they attempted to eliminate.

For reconciliation to take place – as the Truth and Reconciliation Commission in South Africa has shown for crimes much less severe – the government in Rwanda believes there first must be a collective profession of guilt. 'Do we want the truth to be known? Do we want impunity to be punished?' asks Mr. Mucyo, himself a Tutsi genocide survivor.

Whether the *gacaca* system, which is scheduled to start in January (2000), will actually induce Rwanda's Hutu population into a collective admission of responsibility after what is bound to be a traumatic process of recollection is a question neither the government nor the people of Rwanda can answer.

One Western observer in Kigali points out that most Hutus were involved with genocide in some capacity. 'Placing a *genocidaire* – someone who committed genocide – in front of his community will put the community itself through a test of innocence or guilt,' he says.

So far, few Hutus have attempted to come to terms with their guilt, either at individual or collective levels. This is partly because the people they tried to exterminate, the Tutsis, are now firmly in power in Rwanda, and the Hutu fear retaliation. Still, most Hutus have not accepted responsibility for the genocide.

The most common refrain from peasants who admitted killing their Tutsi neighbors is that they did so in the context of the war their (Hutu) government was fighting against the (Tutsi-dominated) Rwandan Patriotic Front."[79]

One highly sensitive subject the Tutsi-dominated regime and the international community never fully addressed, if at all, was to what degree the Tutsi-led Rwandan Patriotic Front (RPF) itself, which went on to form the government after winning the war in 1994, contributed to the genocide of its own people.

When the Tutsi-dominated Rwandan Patriotic Army (RPA) first invaded Rwanda from Uganda on 1 October 1990 – under the leadership of Fred Rwigyema who was killed on the second day of the fighting and was Paul Kagame's close friend since childhood – they sent a wave of fear, and even panic, throughout the country among the Hutu who were afraid that their former rulers were coming back to reconquer them, take their land and property and oppress them again.

It was mostly a myth. But it was a myth that was deeply embedded in the collective psyche of the Hutu majority. The Hutu government and elite capitalised on this fear and attempted to radicalise it into mass hysteria especially when the protracted conflict continued through the early 1990s, forcing the Hutu regime to make major concessions to the RPF under the Arusha Accords signed in neighbouring Tanzania in August 1993 by the Rwandan government and its Tutsi adversaries that called for power sharing.

In the months before the genocide, Rwandan radio broadcasts and Hutu publications inflamed passions among the Hutu, exhorting them to get their weapons ready for a final solution to the Tutsi menace, because of the invasion.

Had the predominantly Tutsi Rwandan Patriotic Army (RPA) – the armed wing of the RPF – not invaded Rwanda, the Hutu would not have been scared into assuming a defensive posture, preparing for war against an invading force that never existed. And many of them, if not the majority, had legitimate fear – vindicated by history – that the Tutsi were indeed coming back to reconquer them, take their land and property and dominate them again as they had done for hundreds of years. And the only way to prevent that from happening again was by wiping them out; a logic of madness first used and officially sanctioned by the Hutu government and other members of the Hutu elite.

The Hutu were, of course, again vindicated in their belief about the re-imposition of Tutsi domination, as the victorious Rwandan Patriotic Front (RPF), dominated by Tutsis, did exactly that when it went on to form a government that was predominantly Tutsi, excluding the Hutu majority from meaningful representation.

Therefore, by invading Rwanda, the Ugandan-based Tutsis contributed to the genocide of their own people in a very significant way the Tutsi-dominated regime in Kigali would rather not acknowledge, and for understandable reasons. It led the invasion, when it was still a rebel group (RPF), and was therefore partly responsible for what happened in Rwanda from October 1990 all the way down to the genocide and beyond.

None of that would have happened had the invasion not taken place. It did not happen in 32 years since independence when they Hutu were in power. They did not try to exterminate the Tutsi during all those years. So why, all of a sudden, would have they tried to do so in 1994? There would have been nothing to inflame passions among the Hutu and trigger the genocide had they not been invaded by the Tutsi from Uganda.

And had any Tutsi group, not just the RPF, invaded Rwanda before 1990 – in the eighties or even in the seventies – from any of the neighbouring countries posing a credible military threat to the Hutu regime in Kigali, the results would probably have been the same. The Hutu would have reacted violently against the Tutsi.

The Hutu majority would have panicked, afraid that the Tutsi were on their way back to take over the country and dominate them again. And they probably would have massacred tens of thousands of Tutsis, at least thousands of them, and may be even hundreds of thousands, to make sure they don't get the chance to seize power and subjugate the Hutu again.

The RPF was also guilty of genocide against the Hutu, not only in Congo where it went on a search-and-destroy mission in hot pursuit of the perpetrators of the 1994 massacres and ended up killing more than 200,000 Hutu civilians who sought refuge there, but also within Rwanda itself where the Tutsi-dominated army killed thousands of Hutu civilians, for example, 5,000 of them in 1995 at Kibeho alone; pogroms which could justifiably be used to bring charges of genocide against the predominantly Tutsi government before an international war crimes tribunal as crimes against humanity.

The Tutsi-dominated Rwandan Patriotic Front which seized power in 1994 when it stopped the genocide also contributed to that holocaust by refusing to withdraw its forces from Rwanda after it invaded the country from Uganda, knowing full well that the invasion would trigger a defensive and retaliatory response from the Hutu government and lead to escalation of the conflict. By starting and continuing the war, the RPF showed little interest in a negotiated settlement. It also helped create a hostile environment for the extermination of its own people and provoked an inevitable response from the Hutu who fought back to defend themselves against the invaders.

Glossing over these facts will not change history.

The reconciliation process even in the traditional context[80] can not begin in earnest, let alone succeed, unless the Tutsi-dominated regime itself also acknowledges its role in fomenting trouble which culminated in the 1994 genocide when it was a rebel force fighting to oust the

Hutu government of President Juvénal Habyarimana.

The alternative is continued polarisation and war between the Hutu and the Tutsi especially when the Tutsi rulers insist that it is only the Hutu who should accept responsibility for the genocide, conveniently ignoring the fact that had the Tutsi not invaded Rwanda from Uganda in 1990 in order to try to take over the country, the massacres which were perpetrated almost four years later in 1994 would not even have taken place.

We must apportion guilt accordingly if we are to construct a proportional perspective on reality in the Rwandan post-genocidal context.

International Criminal Tribunal and Betrayal

The 1994 genocide led to the arrest of more than 130,000 people accused or suspected of having participated in the extermination of almost one million Tutsis and their Hutu sympathisers.

It also led to the establishment of the International Criminal Tribunal for Rwanda (ICTR) by the United Nations to handle the most serious offences classified as crimes against humanity. The UN got its mandate from the 1948 Genocide Convention to establish the court.

In September 1998, the UN-supervised tribunal based in Arusha, Tanzania, set precedent when it sentenced Rwanda's former prime minister, Jean Kambanda, a Hutu, to life in prison for his role in the 1994 holocaust. He became the first person in history to be convicted of genocide as defined by the 1948 Genocide Convention after World War II.

And like its counterpart, the International Criminal Tribunal for the former Yugoslavia (Bosnia, etc.), the Rwandan international criminal court evoked memories of the Nuremberg trials after World War II.

The Nuremberg trials were a series of war crimes trials conducted in Nuremberg, West Germany, from 1945 to 1949, by the allied powers who won World War II: the United States, the Soviet Union, Great Britain, and France.

The accused were tried for crimes committed under three categories: Crimes Against Peace – planning and waging aggressive war; War Crimes – murder or mistreatment of civilians or prisoners of war, killing of hostages, plunder of property, wanton destruction of communities; and Crimes Against Humanity – murder, extermination or enslavement of any civilian population before or during a war on political, racial or religious grounds, and expulsion of entire communities or groups of people from their countries on the grounds that they did not "belong" there.

The Nuremberg trials led to the formulation, establishment and implementation of new principles in the law of nations. The most important principle and which, like the rest, the allied powers promised to uphold and implement as a result of the war was the principle of individual responsibility: every person is responsible for his/her own actions and must be punished for those actions if they are wrong under the law of nations as crimes against humanity.

The Genocide Convention was a product of the Nuremberg trials. It was the first time the crime of genocide was defined under that convention.

Under international law, genocide is defined as the willful or intentional and systematic destruction of a group of people or community – whether ethnic, racial, religious, national, cultural, linguistic, historical or whatever – by a government or any other another group that wants to achieve that goal.

Although the term "genocide" was first coined in 1944, the crime of genocide itself has been committed almost in all parts of the world throughout history. The coinage of the term is attributed to Raphael Lemkin, a naturalised

American of Polish origin, whose family was killed by the Nazi during the holocaust.

Lemkin first used the term "genocide" in his book *Axis Rule in Occupied Europe*. He contended that persecution and extermination of Jews and other groups during World War II deserved to be treated as crimes against humanity specifically defined as such under international law. And he campaigned to get countries to agree to pass a law, binding on all nations, that would specifically deal with state-sanctioned terror and other acts targeting particular groups of people for elimination because of what they are.

The UN General Assembly approved the Convention on the Prevention and Punishment of the Crime of Genocide on 9 December 1948. It became the first treaty for human rights proposed by the United Nations for ratification by the member states.

The term "genocide" was first used to describe state-sponsored terror and campaigns for the systematic extermination of Jews and other people in Germany in the 1930s – before the term was coined – and in the 1940s. The Nazis wanted to wipe out the entire Jewish community in Europe. They also wanted to exterminate other people belonging to "undesirable" racial, ethnic and national groups in Eastern Europe.

After Hitler became the leader of Germany in 1933, the city of Nuremberg became the spiritual centre for the Nazis when they held their annual conferences nearby from 1933 to 1938. Nuremberg was also the hometown of Nazi leader Julius Streicher and it became a major operational base for spewing propaganda against the Jews and other groups of people who were considered to be inferior to the "Aryan" race.

In 1935, the National Socialists held a conference in Nuremberg and passed what came to be known as the Nuremberg Laws which deprived German Jews of their citizenship and other rights and forbade intermarriage between Jews and non-Jews. People of partly Jewish descent were also deprived of their rights in a number of areas.

The Nuremberg Laws had striking parallels to the Hutu Ten Commandments published in the virulently anti-Tutsi publication, *Kangura*, in Rwanda, which strictly forbade intermarriage between Hutus and Tutsis in order to maintain the "purity" of the Hutu race, and – together with another Hutu publication *Le Medaille* – called for the extermination of "the Tutsi race," almost identical to what Hitler did to the Jews.

The two publications and radio broadcasts also urged the Hutu to isolate the Tutsi and expel them from the country and send them back to their "original" homeland, Ethiopia, dead or alive:

"Shrill   calls   for   Tutsi   extermination   (were) disseminated via the print and electronic media. Under the editorship of one Hassan Ngeze, the newspaper *Kangura* listed the 'Hutu ten commandments' that decreed social isolation of the 'evil' Tutsis, and abominated cross-ethnic marriage for polluting 'pure Hutu.' 'By the way,' mused the Hutu-edited *La Medaille* magazine in February 1994, 'the Tutsi race could be extinguished.'

The most virulent and effective incitement to hatred and violence, however, was reportedly broadcast by Radio.Television Libre des Mille Collines, and was commissioned by Hutu extremists with official connivance in July 1993.

By early 1994 the Hutu propaganda mill was requesting that its sympathizers 'reach for the hatchet' in order 'to fill the unfilled graves with yet more Tutsi' bodies.

Incitements to kill were spiced with 'history lessons' of 'well-known' Tutsi treachery and exploitation of the Hutus."[81]

The parallels between Nazi Germany in the 1930s and

64

1940s and Rwanda from 1992 to 1994 are frightening. The agenda, isolation and extermination of the targeted group, was the same. Even the language used was almost the same. The virulently anti-Tutsi rhetoric reminded one of the anti-Jewish propaganda under Hitler; so did the intellectual directorate that masterminded the campaign.

Hutu professors in Rwanda used pseudo-intellectual arguments to justify the massacre of the Tutsi, as did Nazi intellectuals to justify the extermination of the Jews. And the death camps where millions of Jews perished in the gas chambers at the hands of the Nazis were no different in intent from the Catholic church compounds and other holy places which became some of the worst massacre sites during the Rwandan holocaust. They included schools, soccer fields, hospitals and clinics and other sanctuaries to which the Tutsi and Hutu moderates fled for safety.

But the parallels between Germany and Rwanda when both nations descended into madness went beyond that and included the establishment of international war crimes tribunals for both.

After World II, Nuremberg became the seat of the international tribunal for war crimes perpetrated in that conflict, the bloodiest in human history up to that time. In 1945, the charter of the Nuremberg Tribunal listed persecution on racial or religious grounds as a crime for which the victorious Allies would try Nazi offenders. It established the principle of individual accountability of government officials who carried out the extermination policies.

The United Nations, in a convention adopted in 1948, defined in detail the crime of genocide and provided for its punishment by competent national courts of the state on whose territory the crime was committed or by an international tribunal.

But the United States refused to ratify the Genocide Convention, contending that it violated national sovereignty especially in its provision calling for the establishment of an international tribunal and in the potential liability of an individual citizen. It was not until 37 years later, in 1986, that the United States finally ratified the convention.

Tragically, it was again the United States which was adamantly opposed to attempts by the United Nations to call the 1994 Rwandan massacres, "genocide." Had the UN defined those pogroms as "genocide," it would have invoked the Genocide Convention, thus obligating member states including the United States to intervene in Rwanda; an intervention that would have entailed commitment of troops including ground forces in combat role, which the United States resolutely opposed, citing the failed UN mission in Somalia where 18 American soldiers and 24 Pakistani peace keepers were killed in 1992 as the reason for opposing such intervention.

But lack of national interest and racism were the main reasons why the United States and other Western powers did not intervene in Rwanda, while they intervened in Bosnia and Kosovo in the former Yugoslavia with full military force to save lives of white people.

The establishment of the International War Crimes Tribunal for Yugoslavia at the Hague in the Netherlands paved the way for the creation of the international criminal tribunal for Rwanda by the UN in November 1994. In fact, the two courts were headed by the same chief prosecutor at the Hague. The international criminal tribunal in the Netherlands also handled appeals from the UN-supervised court in Arusha, Tanzania, which dealt with Rwandan cases, and was therefore the senior of the two courts.

The first defendant to appear before the International Criminal Tribunal for Rwanda (ICTR), Jean-Paul Akayesu, 44 years old, was a former mayor of the central Rwandan town of Taba. He was charged with genocide, inciting genocide, rape, crimes against humanity, murder and torture. He pleaded not guilty on all counts.

Among the people who testified against him was Major-General Romeo Dallaire who was the commander of the UN peacekeeping troops in Rwanda known as the United Nations Assistance Mission in Rwanda (UNAMIR). He remained in Rwanda with his small, weak force during the genocide. Akayesu was charged with the deaths of at least 2,000 Tutsis. According to a report from Arusha, Tanzania, in *The Boston Globe*:

"Akayesu...has pleaded not guilty to 12 charges of genocide, crimes against humanity, murder and torture. Now in its second year, his trial is the first before the International Criminal Tribunal for Rwanda....

In January (1998), the UN Secretary General Kofi Annan authorized Dallaire to testify before the tribunal, but the United Nations has emphasized that it does not want a trial of the UN mission in Rwanda or of the foreign governments involved. The United Nations previously refused to allow Dallaire to appear before a Belgian legislative inquiry into the deaths of 10 Belgian peacekeepers under his command."[82]

In his testimony before the international tribunal, Dallaire blamed the international community for its unwillingness to stop the massacres in Rwanda:

"It seems to me unimaginable that everyday we saw people being massacred and yet (the international community) folded its arms....

There were slogans against Tutsis which were beyond imagination. [The Rwandan Patriotic Front (RPF) were] portrayed as having the eyes and teeth of devils...that they ate children.

The country, a country and people for whom I have the greatest respect, is mainly of people who live traditionally, respecting authority without question. If this was enlightened, it works well. But when it is used for evil...well, we saw the consequences."[83]

Rwanda is a highly hierarchical society, a characteristic that has been used by some people to explain why so many Hutu peasants participated in the massacres: They were simply obeying orders, from the government and its functionaries, without question in a society where people simply followed orders.

Even the Roman Catholic Church in Rwanda is virtually a government unto itself with enormous influence over the people. Had the clergy taken a stand against the genocide, as some clergymen and nuns did at the expense of their lives, many people would have listened to them and a lot of lives would have been saved.

Yet all this unconditional submission to authority that amounts to subservience still does not explain why many people in the rural areas – where the church and traditional authority is strongest – participated in the massacres willingly, and why they even killed their own Tutsi relatives and friends and neighbours with whom they had lived for years without any hostility between them. Part of the answer is that there was hidden anger and hostility towards the Tutsi even if they were their neighbours and relatives. It also partly explains the complex pattern of relations between the two ethnic groups through the centuries.

There was deep-seated prejudice and mistrust between the two, however latent it may have been, that was reinforced by stereotypes and which was only waiting to be exploited and galvanised into a potent force by unscrupulous elements within the Rwandan society in pursuit of their own agenda. The agenda turned out to be genocide in the quest for Hutu supremacy and "eternal paradise" in a country cleansed of all Tutsis who were collectively denounced as the embodiment of evil in the Rwandan context. It was precisely these unscrupulous elements for whom the International Criminal Tribunal for

Rwanda was established to deal with, because of their prime role in orchestrating the massacres.

Major-General Dalliare's testimony before the tribunal was significant not only in highlighting the failure of the international community to intervene in Rwanda and stop the genocide, and in building the case against Akayesu and the other defendants on the trial; it also underscored the fragility of the peace accords signed in Tanzania in August 1993 by the Rwandan Hutu government and the Tutsi-dominated Rwandan Patriotic Front (RPF).

The majority of the people in President Juvénal Habyarimana's Hutu government were no more interested in forming a coalition government than their Tutsi adversaries were. It was only a temporary arrangement and a marriage of convenience for both.

Neither side had the slightest doubt about each other's intentions, as both vied for supremacy, waiting for the best opportunity to strike or make a move and outmanoeuvre the other out of power.

Therefore when Dallaire's UN peacekeeping force (UNAMIR) was sent to Rwanda in September 1993 to oversee the implementation of the peace agreement known as the Arusha Accords, it went on a mission that had little chance of succeeding, sabotaged from the beginning by the very same people – the parties to the agreement – who were supposedly interested in seeing it accomplished. And when the massacres started, the international community only compounded the felony by looking the other way, the biggest culprits being the permanent UN Security Council members – the Big Five: the United States, Russia, the United Kingdom, France and China – who had the power to authorise intervention in Rwanda and stop the killings. As Charles Paul Freund stated in *Reason*:

"In Rwanda, President Clinton took no action at all to forestall the true genocide that occurred five years ago, although the United States, France, and Belgium were all forewarned that many thousands of persons would soon be hacked to death by their traditional tribal enemies."[84]

Even after the International Criminal Tribunal for Rwanda (ICTR) was established, the major powers did not do as much as they could and should have to provide the resources needed to enable the court to fulfill its mandate or to apprehend suspects wanted for trial. And as Major-General Dallaire said in his testimony before the tribunal in Tanzania on 25 February 1998, the 1994 massacres could have been stopped if a small, well-armed UN force (of about 5,000 soldiers) had been sent in early for that purpose as he had repeatedly requested.[85]

Yet the atrocities were perpetrated in full glare, with cameras of the international media focused on them for a whole three months. In spite of all this exposure in the international spotlight, no one tried to rescue the victims:

"General Dallaire...(told the) UN tribunal that 'with a well-armed force of 5,000 men and the proper mandate, 'the UN could have stopped the slaughter of hundreds of thousands of Rwandans....

It seems inconceivable that one can watch...thousands of people being...massacred...everyday in the media and remain passive,' the former United Nations Assistance Mission for Rwanda (UNAMIR) commander said as his voice broke and tears fell from his eyes."[86]

General Dallaire was summoned to the court by Akayesu's defence lawyers as part of a strategy to dilute or minimise their client's guilt. If the United Nations was unable to stop the genocide, as they hoped Dallaire would testify, how could one have expected Akayesu, an individual, to stop the massacres?

It sounded like a clever argument. But Akayesu was not blamed for all the massacres or for the genocide in Rwanda which the UN could have prevented or stopped.

He was blamed for the killings which took place in his jurisdiction over which he had authority. And he did nothing to stop them.

Akayesu was charged with more than merely standing by as thousands of people, mostly Tutsi, were slaughtered, doing nothing to stop the massacres. The charges he faced spanned the entire spectrum of crimes under the Genocide Convention, ranging from rape to inciting genocide and crimes against humanity. And Dallaire, of course, said the UN had the power and the means to stop the genocide but did nothing. As he stated during his testimony:

"The question is whether a well-equipped force with the proper mandate could have stopped civilians armed with knives and machetes, and I say absolutely, in one week....It was an unimaginable exercise in frustration. The UN was passive before the massacres."[87]

The Hutu national government would not have accepted an intervention force. But the UN could have invoked powers conferred upon it under the rules of engagement that specifically allowed the use of force "to stop or prevent crimes against humanity." Dallaire said he made this point repeatedly as the massacres spread beyond the capital Kigali and genocide leaders travelled to the remotest corners of the country urging Hutu peasants to do what they were supposed to do, and telling them they were "behind their work," thus encouraging them to kill the Tutsi even faster.

Tragically, after the Tutsi took over the country, they turned the tables and went on to perpetrate similar atrocities which included brutal measures to starve Hutus into submission by destroying their crops and burning their homes. According to a report from Gisenyi, northwestern Rwanda, in *The Christian Science Monitor*:

"Tutsi leaders ordered banana plantations near Gisenyi

71

(the capital of Gisenyi Province) destroyed so they couldn't provide cover for Hutu rebels.

More than 10,000 people have died since May (1997) in rebel attacks and Tutsi Army reprisals in the northwest (Gisenyi and Ruhengeri provinces)....

The Hutu insurgents, a highly mobile force..., have successfully turned the northwestern provinces into war zones, accentuating ethnic cleavages in other parts of the country. Analysts say the history of the region accounts for some of the support. More than 50 percent of the former Hutu political establishment – and 80 percent of the former armed forces – came from the northwest. Many of them played a key role in the genocide....

(The insurgents) are fed, sheltered, and hardly ever denounced by local citizens.

While it is true that the rebels are in the habit of taking at gunpoint whatever is not offered, there have been surprising demonstrations of loyalty. More disturbingly, there have been collective displays of solidarity during and after rebel attacks. One such display came during (an) attack (on a bus). Hutu peasants surrounded the bus and burst into songs of Hutu supremacy as 35 people were massacred."[88]

Hutu leaders who were being tried by the International Criminal Tribunal for Rwanda (ICTR) in Tanzania were some of the very same people who provided inspiration for this continuing rebellion.

They were undoubtedly war criminals and deserved to be punished for what they did during the genocide. But regardless of how much one may disagree with them, and however reprehensible their acts, we must confront one harsh reality. Many Hutu civilians, and not just the rebels, saw them as leaders in the struggle for the rights of the Hutu majority. And unless the Hutu majority are won over by the Tutsi-dominated government through genuine concessions, Rwanda shall remain a nation divided even if it continues to exist – although it can not effectively function – as one country. Its split identity as a dual entity with irreconcilable parts is a recipe for catastrophe.

If the Tutsi minority rulers refuse to make significant concessions to the powerless Hutu majority, the only other options will be continuation of war, with no end in sight, or separation of Gisenyi and Ruhengeri provinces – the two Hutu strongholds – from the rest of Rwanda to form a nucleus of an independent Hutu state.

A way must be found to accommodate the interests of the Hutu majority if Rwanda is to survive as a nation and not merely as an ethnic cauldron. As one analyst, Scot Straus, remarked:

"Whether this (Tutsi-dominated) government likes it or not, the constituency it should be worrying about are the Hutus. They make up over 85 percent of the country. If the government doesn't find a way of bringing them on board, this cycle of violence will never end."[89]

The International Criminal Tribunal for Rwanda was not given the mandate to end this cycle of violence. But even if it had been, it would not have succeeded, given the magnitude and complexity of the problem.

Only a national referendum under UN supervision or some other internationally supervised plebiscite, asking the Hutu and the Tutsi how they want to be governed and if they want to separate, can help resolve the conflict.

In spite of its shortcomings and failures with regard to Rwanda, especially its refusal to intervene to stop the genocide, The United Nations still set a good precedent when it established the international tribunal for war crimes committed during the 1994 Rwandan genocide. And by doing so, it may be encouraged to take another step and propose a referendum to end the Rwandan conflict through creative destruction – dissolution of the current Rwandan nation and creation of two sovereign entities of Hutuland and Tutsiland as ethnostates – as it did in the case of Ethiopia which led to the independence of Eritrea in 1993, although Eritrea was already a separate country and was only forcibly incorporated into Ethiopia; and as it tried to do in the case of Morocco and Western Sahara by asking Western Saharans to decide in a plebiscite whether or not they wanted to be absorbed by – or become an integral part of – Morocco.

The UN set another precedent when it instituted the international court for the Rwandan war crimes. It made a commendable effort towards creating a permanent international criminal tribunal with the mandate to handle war crimes committed in all countries around the world, although it will probably be years before this goal is realised, if at all. But it is a step in the right direction and has underscored the imperative need for such a tribunal even if one is never established. As Kingsley Moghalu, a legal adviser to the International Criminal Tribunal for Rwanda (ICTR), said in anticipation of the genocide convictions: "Our judgments will detail genocide: We will provide the legal lamppost for future generations."[90]

Convictions of the accused on charges of genocide by the International Criminal Tribunal for Rwanda will be in sharp contrast with what happened at Nuremberg. None of the 22 Nazi leaders at the Nuremberg trials were convicted of genocide. The definition of the crime of genocide came later, after the Nuremberg trials.

Men like Hans Frank, the mass murderer and governor-general of Nazi-occupied Poland, and Rudolph Hess, were charged with crimes against peace, crimes of war, and halfway through the trials, with crimes against humanity. Hess, who was Hitler's deputy from 1933 – 1939, eventually became the only inmate in Berlin's Spandau prison. He was convicted to life imprisonment.

That was also the maximum sentence the Rwandan war crimes tribunal based in neighbouring Tanzania could impose under its UN mandate, a restriction that rankled

Rwandan officials who wanted the death penalty imposed for the most serious crimes.

The first person to be convicted, Akayesu, was a relatively minor figure compared with Theoneste Bagosora, the former Rwandan army chief and senior official at the defence ministry who opened the armoury and distributed weapons and ammunition to the perpetrators of the genocide. He was in custody in Tanzania together with Akayesu and other defendants.

But Akayesu's trial was critical, nonetheless, in establishing credibility for the court. As one defence lawyer at the trial put it: "Comparatively speaking, Akayesu is a nobody. But because of that, the prosecution has had to work much harder to prove him guilty of genocide."[91]

The court was also criticised for being slow and sloppy in its work. But as the tribunal's president, Judge Laity Kama of Senegal, explained, the imperatives of justice were partly to blame:

"We have to abide by the rules of evidence and avoid expeditious justice at all costs. The same people that are pressuring us today will accuse us tomorrow saying, 'This is what African justice amounts to.'"[92]

By codifying legal enormities such as genocide, the court paved the way for the establishment of a permanent war crimes tribunal which would also have precedent to draw upon because of the work done in Arusha, Tanzania, where the Rwandan war crimes tribunal was based. In the words of Pascal Besnier, a defence lawyer with the court:

"History will retain the analytical work done by magistrates and not the administrative headaches of this tribunal. There is a sense here that we are working for the betterment of humanism."[93]

But some observers did not share that glossy assessment. One was Betty Murungi, a lawyer based in Nairobi, Kenya, working for the Coalition for the International Criminal Tribunal that was pushing for the establishment of a permanent world court. As she stated: "The Akayesu ruling will be a fairly momentous one, but let us not imagine for one minute that it will affect international law to such a vast extent. Akayesu will not constitute the perfect precedent."[94]

She went on to explain that the witnesses produced by the prosecution were not the most credible because the tribunal could not guarantee their safety. She did, however, concede the importance of the proceedings: "What this will do is send the message that genocide is not acceptable and hopefully expedite the establishment of an international tribunal."[95]

That is because there was no question that genocide had taken place in Rwanda. Therefore in that sense, the international criminal tribunal in Arusha, Tanzania, set an important precedent, imposing sentence for genocide for the first time in recorded history.

But the court also became embroiled in conflict and, according to some observers including the staunchly partisan Rwandan officials for perfectly understandable reasons, impaired its credibility when it decided on 18 March 1999 to free a former Rwandan army officer suspected of involvement in the killings of 10 Belgian peace keepers. Prosecutors had asked that the charge of crimes against humanity, unrelated to the deaths of the Belgian soldiers, be dropped against Major Bernard Ntuyahaga and that he be handed over to Belgium for prosecution.[96]

The three-judge panel at the International Criminal Tribunal for Rwanda (ICTR) ruled that the court did not have the authority to turn a suspect over for prosecution in another country. But it agreed to drop the charges against Bernard Ntuyahaga who once was a major in the Rwanda

Armed Forces (*Forces Rwandaises de Défense* – RDF).

Belgian authorities asked Tanzania to extradite him to Belgium where he was wanted for the assassination of Rwandan Prime Minister Agathe Uwilingiyimana, a Hutu moderate, and for the massacre of 10 Belgian UN peace keepers in Kigali on 7 April 1994, less than a day after the genocide started in the nation's capital.[97] As Keith Richburg, writing about the massacres, stated in his book, *Out of America: A Black Man Confronts Africa*:

"I must admit, I too found it hard to believe the scope of the horror, not even when the initial stories of the atrocities started filtering back to Nairobi (where Keith Richburg was based as the Africa bureau chief of *The Washington Post*). Like the story of bodies piled up six feet high outside Kigali's main hospital. Or the story of the ten Belgian paratroopers who were executed while trying to protect Rwanda's prime minister (a Hutu moderate, Agathe Uwilingiyimana); first they had their Achilles tendons cut to prevent them from escaping, then they were castrated and the severed organs shoved into their mouths.

These were the stories, repeated over and over again, and I didn't believe them. But now I was seeing it with my own eyes. It could no longer be denied."[98]

The killing of the Belgian soldiers precipitated the departure of UN peacekeeping troops from Rwanda, officially signalling the abandonment of the Rwandan holocaust victims by the international community. As Josephine Murebwayire told American President Bill Clinton on his visit to Rwanda on 25 March 1998: "My six children, my husband and two brothers were all killed."[99] Another survivor, Venuste Karasira, told him: "We died because we were left by the United Nations soldiers."[100] And Bill Clinton conceded:

"It may seem strange to you here, especially the many

of you who lost members of your family. But all over the world there were people like me sitting in offices who did not fully appreciate the depth and the speed with which you were being engulfed by this unimaginable terror. We did not immediately call these crimes by their rightful name – genocide....(The killers did their work) five times as fast as the mechanized gas chambers used by the Nazis."[101]

Yet all that meant nothing to the rest of the world as Rwandans, mostly Tutsis, continued to be slaughtered at the rate of more than 8,000 per day, with pictures of piled-up and bloated bodies – on church compounds, at hospitals, on the streets, and floating in rivers – filling television screens in millions of homes round the globe everyday for three months. As Gloriosa Uwimpuhwe, one of the genocide survivors who met with President Clinton, bluntly put it: "There are killings still going on in the country. But the international community is not reacting against that."[102] It never intended to.

President Clinton was one of the leaders who knew – from the CIA and the DIA (United States Defence Intelligence Agency) and other intelligence sources – that the Tutsi were about to be massacred by the Hutu.

In fact, before the genocide started, France, Belgium, Italy and the United States all had troops in the region – some of them even had troops in Kigali or nearby – with enough military equipment, who could easily have intervened to avert the catastrophe. Instead, they only evacuated their people knowing full well, from their intelligence services, that a holocaust was imminent.[103]

Compounding the felony was the unwillingness or reluctance of some Western countries to extradite to Tanzania the perpetrators of the genocide to be tried by the International Criminal Tribunal for Rwanda (ICTR). Rwandan officials were even more anxious to get the suspects and try them in Rwandan courts where those found guilty of the most heinous crimes could be sentenced to death, unlike in Tanzania where the maximum sentence the international war crimes tribunal could impose was life imprisonment. As Rwandan President Pasteur Bizimungu, in a ceremony to commemorate the 1994 genocide and end a week of mourning, said about the difficulty his country faced in bringing the suspects to justice:

"Here in Rwanda, we do not bear any grudge against Europe. But I want to also point out that it was the Europeans who are responsible for this type of chaos we have here....People who were leading the genocide are free in Europe. Europe must bring them to book....I see the Canadian ambassador here. Canada should extradite Leon Mugesera."[104]

Mugesera was a key aide to the late President Juvénal Habyarimana, hence a critical player in the 1994 genocide, wanted by the international war crimes court in Tanzania. His extradition was necessary as a quest for justice and as an integral part of the judicial proceedings. But it could not mitigate the enormity of the crime of willful neglect of the Rwandan holocaust victims by the international community, especially by the major powers who had the means to stop it. As Yael S. Aronoff, former assistant for regional humanitarian affairs in the United States Defence Department's Office of Humanitarian and Refugee Affairs in the Clinton Administration, stated:

"Once genocide is under way, it is unlikely that anything but military force will end the horror. The main question the president needs to address is, 'Do you support military action by U.N. forces, and by U.S. forces when the United Nations is not acting quickly enough to stop genocide already underway?'

In his recent speech to the Rwandans, President

Clinton highlighted three claims: first, that he did not fully appreciate the depth and speed of the genocide; second, that his administration should have called the killings 'genocide' earlier; third, that the United States should have acted more quickly to stop the genocide and not have allowed the refugee camps to become safe havens for the perpetrators.

While working in the secretary of defense's Office of Humanitarian and Refugee Affairs, I participated in the Department of Defense Rwanda Task Force. I had the stomach-turning task of sending daily body counts to my bosses every morning, and thus I can attest to the fact that the intelligence was there for anyone in the administration to see....

Even after the administration did begin using the term genocide, very little action was taken....

It is a positive suggestion to have the administration and the international community improve its system for identifying nations in danger of genocidal violence, but, as is clear here, information was and is not the main problem. It is the political will to act on that information that is lacking. I witnessed this lack of will.

Despite lobbying by myself and others, even suggestions about interference with the radio broadcasts inciting the killing were discouraged by some in the Defense Department – not to mention suggestions about speeding up equipment for U.N. volunteers or sending U.S. soldiers to put a stop to the massacres....

I do not think that there was a Principals' Meeting on Rwanda during the entire two-and-a-half months in which the genocide was taking place."[105]

Aronoff's testimony was corroborated by others. James Woods, who was assistant secretary at the United States Defence Department from 1986 to 1994, said on the American Public Broadcasting System (PBS) series, *Frontline*, on 26 January 1999 that he was asked in 1993

80

to list possible serious crises that the Clinton Administration might be confronted with. He said he drew up a list on which he included Rwanda. "But higher authorities told him to take it (Rwanda) off because American interests were not involved."[106] The suppression continued.

At the end of April 1994, the State Department conceded in a secret intelligence report that the massacres which had just taken place in Rwanda amounted to genocide. But Tony Marley who then worked as a consultant at the State Department said on the same television programme *Frontline* that an official in the Clinton Administration warned that the Democratic Party could lose votes in the coming congressional elections if President Clinton, a Democrat, admitted that "genocide was taking place in Rwanda and yet be seen to do nothing about it." At one point, Marley even recommended that the American military should use electronic gear to jam inflammatory radio transmissions from the two Hutu-controlled radio stations in Rwanda urging Hutus to kill Tutsis. But a lawyer from the American Defence Department dismissed the idea, insisting that such a move would violate the First Amendment.[107]

He was, of course, referring to the amendment to the American constitution which guarantees freedom of expression. How that was relevant in the Rwandan context during that period when genocide was taking place was never fully explained. He was defending the Hutus' right to free speech, which amounted to incitement to genocide by Hutu radio broadcasts, in a country where the Tutsi did not even have the right to life.

Even when Rwanda was overflowing with corpses, televised worldwide, everyday for almost three months straight, the American ambassador to the United Nations, Madeleine Albright who went on to become U.S. Secretary of State under President Clinton, effectively blocked a UN Security Council debate and a vote on the genocide taking place Rwanda. It was a deliberate policy decision by the Clinton Administration not to intervene and stop the genocide; it was also one of the most racist, and most selfish, the United States has ever made in its history. A simple news report on the radio that American troops were on the way to Rwanda – let alone the arrival of soldiers landing on Rwandan soil – would have scared many Hutu extremists who were on the genocidal rampage. Many of them would not have continued with the killings and many lives would have been saved.

The unwillingness by the United States and other major powers as well as the rest of the world to intervene and stop the genocide sent one clear message to African victims of war and persecution: "When you desperately need help, don't expect the international community to come to your rescue even when you are dying in front of cameras. You are on your own."

Condemnation of atrocities is not enough. Actions speak louder than words. The genocide may have scarred the conscience of the world, but it did not jolt mankind into action. The world was morally obliged to intervene. Instead, race, probably even more than national interest, was given priority and became the paramount factor in the decision by the United States and other world powers not to intervene.

If millions of whites were being slaughtered in South Africa, the United States and other white nations would have intervened right away to save them. They would not even talking about national interest. They would be concerned about saving lives of white victims – whether or not there was any national interest involved.

Finally, after the fact, with one million people dead, the international community tried to salvage its conscience by establishing the war crimes tribunal for Rwanda under UN auspices to punish some of the perpetrators of the genocide, especially those who engineered the holocaust.

The most prominent political figure to be convicted

was former Rwandan Prime Minister Jean Kambanda. On 1 May 1994, Kambanda appeared before the international war crimes tribunal in Arusha, Tanzania, and pleaded guilty to the charges that he orchestrated the massacre of thousands of Tutsis and moderate Hutus. This was the tribunal's first conviction since it was formed three years before.[108]

UN Secretary-General Kofi Annan, an African himself and a native of Ghana, was travelling in Africa around the same time when Kambanda pleaded guilty. He became the target of strong criticism for failing to intervene in Rwanda during the genocide when he was in charge of the UN peacekeeping forces worldwide:

"Add UN Secretary-General Kofi Annan to the list of senior world leaders who knew in advance of the Rwandan genocide but did nothing to stop it, the *New Yorker* magazine reports. Citing a former deputy (of Annan) and related documents, the magazine says Annan...ordered his forces in Rwanda not to intervene in plans by the Hutu-led government to slaughter minority Tutsis."[109]

A number of people knew that high-ranking UN officials were aware of the Rwandan Hutu regime's agenda to exterminate the Tutsi, but few believed that it was Annan who ordered the UN peacekeeping troops not to intervene. In an interview with *60 Minutes* on CBS, an American television programme, in early 2000, Annan defended himself by contending that he approached 150 governments, requesting them to intervene in Rwanda. He said none agreed to do so. And he blamed the major powers – more than anybody else – for not having the political will to intervene and stop the massacres.

Yet he gave no reason why he did not go public with the information he had on the impending catastrophe in Rwanda. People would have understood that he wanted or tried to do something about the situation but couldn't because he was powerless. Simply saying he did not have the power to do anything or that his hands were tied is not enough of an explanation.

Also, a fax copy from UN headquarters obtained by *The New Yorker* showed the order not to intervene came from Annan. May be that is because he had no other choice. He did not have the power to force anyone or any country to send troops to Rwanda to stop the genocide; he was no more than an international civil servant whose execution of duties depended on the willingness of different governments around the world to fulfill his requests. They are the ones who constitute the international community in their official capacity as representatives of their people at the UN and in other international forums and organisations. They knew what was going on in Rwanda even before the massacres started. According to *The Boston Globe*:

"Annan was the head of the UN peacekeeping operations on January 11, 1994, when the commander of the UN forces in Rwanda, General Romeo Dallaire, warned the world body that the Kigali government was planning to slaughter Tutsi and called for intervention.

In a fax sent to UN headquarters in New York, Dallaire quoted a senior Rwandan security official as saying he had been ordered to register all Tutsi in Kigali for the purpose, he suspected, of 'their extermination.'

In reply, Annan's office ordered Dallaire not to protect the informant or follow through on plans to confiscate illegal arms stockpiles. Annan was aware of the order, said his aide, Iqbal Riza, who signed the response.

'I was responsible,' Riza, still Annan's deputy, told *The New Yorker* when shown a copy of the order. 'This is not to say that Mr. Annan was oblivious of what was going on. No. Part of my responsibility was to keep him informed.'

UN officials previously have blocked probes to determine who saw the fax and who issued the order."[110]

Defence lawyers at the Rwandan war crimes tribunal in Tanzania said anyone implicated in the genocide, including Kofi Annan for his unwillingness or failure (or inability) to intervene during the massacres, should be subpoened to testify in order to mitigate or even exonerate their clients. But diplomatic immunity shielded him and other UN officials from testifying.

Annan dismissed as "an old story" the report in *The New Yorker* that – as chief of the UN peacekeeping operations – he failed to intervene in Rwanda during the 1994 genocide, contending that the UN lacked the support of member governments to prevent the massacres.[111] He went on to say, "the failure to prevent the 1994 genocide was local, national and international," and added that the failure included important nations with the power to make a difference.[112] Speaking in Nairobi, Kenya, 4 May 1998, during his eight-nation African trip, Annan also said: "No one can deny that the world failed the people of Rwanda. But the crucial issue is not how to apportion blame with the benefit of hindsight."[113]

Annan made a valid point when he said powerful countries could have made a difference. The American, Belgian and French embassies in Kigali were told immediately about the warning by the Hutu informer and General Dallaire that the Tutsi were about to be exterminated. UN officials also admitted that they received a briefing on the matter. And the same officials and independent experts said the Clinton Administration effectively blocked international involvement for months even after the killings had begun to run their destructive course.

Nothing was done.

The Rwandan war crimes tribunal should have been given an expanded mandate to probe the matter and hold all those involved fully accountable for their actions even if some of them could not be prosecuted because they were protected by diplomatic immunity. But they should have been exposed. And if possible, their diplomatic immunity should have been lifted to force them to testify and even to be punished by the international court.

Otherwise selective dispensation of justice involving only Rwandan officials responsible for orchestrating the massacres could be construed, even if wrongly, as malicious vindictiveness against individuals who are not as influential in international circles as UN officials are. Some of the UN officials were guilty of willful neglect – hence partly responsible for the genocide – even if not as much as the perpetrators of the genocide were, including the Rwandan officials who instigated the holocaust.

The criterion employed was, of course, entitlement to diplomatic immunity which the United Nations invoked to protect its employees such as Kofi Annan from testifying in – let alone from being punished by – the Rwandan war crimes tribunal. But it also impaired the credibility of the UN as an impartial international organisation committed to justice based on universally valid principles which don't discriminate against anybody.

But for such principles to be applicable in the international context, leaders of other countries who blocked intervention in Rwanda during the genocide should have been charged with violating the Genocide Convention – whose invocation by the UN would have mandated military intervention by the member states – and brought before the International Criminal Tribunal for Rwanda (in its expanded form giving it more powers), or before another international tribunal which should have been established by the United Nations (even if only as a temporary court) and specifically charged with handling war crimes.

One of the defendants would definitely have been the American ambassador to the UN, Madeleine Albright (and by extension the United States itself), who was adamantly opposed to international intervention in Rwanda and refused to call the massacres "genocide"; an acknowledgement which would have triggered the Genocide Convention compelling the United States and other countries – as signatories to the treaty – to intervene militarily and stop the massacres.

In spite of its limited mandate, for example not being allowed to impose the death penalty let alone prosecute UN officials and government leaders of other countries for blocking intervention in Rwanda during the genocide, the war crimes tribunal won praise from Kofi Annan on his visit to Arusha, Tanzania, during which he said he hoped the world had learned an important lesson, that mass killers would not go unpunished:

"I hope the message that comes out of this court, to the entire African continent and beyond, is that the days when one was...getting away when you killed hundreds, thousands, are over, that impunity is not going to be allowed to stand."[114]

Annan was in the court when a former military commander, Anatole Nsengiyumya, 47, a Hutu, asked the International Criminal Tribunal for Rwanda (ICTR) to drop an indictment against him on charges of genocide and crimes against humanity. Nsengiyumya served as commander in the northwestern Rwandan town of Gisenyi, the provincial capital, where he was accused of presiding over a meeting in which he ordered Hutus to organise the killing of Tutsis.[115]

The cordial reception Annan was accorded in Tanzania was in sharp contrast with what he was given in Rwanda where he was snubbed by government officials and blamed for not helping prevent the 1994 genocide. He told Rwandans on 7 May 1998 that the world had failed them by not intervening to stop the massacres. But Rwanda's main leaders said his apology was not strong enough and snubbed him by not attending a reception for him.

Presidential spokesman Joseph Bideri called Annan's speech "extremely arrogant, insensitive, and insulting to the Rwandan people."[116]

The purpose of Annan's visit to Rwanda was to restore good relations between the United Nations and the embattled East African country that was abandoned by the international community during the genocide.

In a speech to the Rwandan parliament, Annan admitted that mistakes were made by the international community, and added: "The world must deeply repent this failure."[117] But his remarks did not mollify Rwandan officials who insisted that individuals be held accountable for the decisions which ended in the outbreak of the holocaust; a pointed reference to Annan himself because of his position during that time as head of the UN peacekeeping operations. It was in that capacity that he was accused of having given orders to the peacekeeping troops in Rwanda not to intervene and seize weapons from Hutu extremists before the massacres started.

In response to the speech, Rwandan President Pasteur Bizimungu, Vice President and Defence Minister as well as Rwanda's *de facto* ruler Paul Kagame, and Prime Minister Pierre Celestin Rwigema, boycotted a reception they were to hold for Annan. As presidential spokesman Bideri said: "(Annan) talked of the need for Rwandans to atone, yet he cannot atone for the failure of the UN in Rwanda, which led to to the slaughter of Rwandans."[118]

Not only was the UN peacekeeping force (UNAMIR) in the capital Kigali ordered not to intervene before and even after the massacres started; the UN Security Council cut the size of the force from 2,500 to 250. Yet the commander of the UN peacekeeping troops in Rwanda, General Dallaire, told UN headquarters in an emergency plea that he would need 5,000 soldiers, twice the original number, for a successful preemptive strike against Hutu militias and seize weapons from them before they started the genocide.

Therefore reducing the number of the UN peace troops to 250 – when 20 times as many soldiers would be needed to prevent the holocaust – was a direct slap in the face of General Dallaire and the intended victims of the genocide. It amounted to saying, "You are on your own. The rest of the world does not care about you. Die."

So, it is easy to understand why Rwandan leaders were very offended by Annan's speech, and why the victims of genocide felt betrayed by the international community which should have protected them.

Rwanda's Foreign Minister Anastase Gasana acknowledged that Annan had often cited "a lack of political will" for the United Nation's inability to act, but said: "We want to know who was behind this lack of political will."[119] With Annan sitting beside him in Rwanda's parliament, Gasana bitterly criticised the United Nations and its predecessor, the League of Nations, for its bad treatment of Rwanda since 1922. He demanded compensation for the genocide and underscored the refusal by the United Nations to use its troops in Rwanda – as repeatedly requested by General Dallaire – to stop the massacres at a time when Anna himself was head of the UN peacekeeping operations.

At a question-and-answer session with Rwandan members of parliament, Annan said he had not expected such sharp criticism but cited the adage that "the guest is always the prisoner of the host," a remark that drew laughter from the legislators and others in the National Assembly. He went to say: "I did not regret what I did, but I do regret that we could not get more help for Rwanda."[120] He also said he was on a mission "to help heal the wounds and divisions that still torment Rwanda," but restoring trust and security was ultimately up to Rwandans. "You and only you can show the world that there is life even after genocide, love even after hate, humanity even after evil."[121]

Other UN officials accompanying Annan on his

African trip said they were not surprised by the outpouring of anger and bitter denunciations of the United Nations and the international community. As UN spokesman Fred Eckhard remarked: "These people have been through a lot, they have a lot of anger to vent. The secretary general has become their lightning rod."[122]

Survivors of the Rwandan genocide also expressed their anger and bitter resentment towards the United Nations and said Annan bore heavy responsibility for the 1994 massacres. In an open letter to Annan, the genocide survivors group Ibuka said the UN decision to pull out the peacekeeping troops when the genocide started led to a horrendous tragedy:

"In taking that unfortunate decision to pull out its blue helmets, the UN condemned almost 1.5 million people to certain death. This act is considered without doubt an offense of non-assistance to a people in danger and yourself and the organization you head up bear a heavy responsibility."[123]

The statement was signed by Jean-Bosco Rutagengwa, president of the Ibuka group. It expressed the collective sentiment not only of the survivors but also of those who perished in the holocaust and who would have lived had the international community intervened to stop the massacres. Its refusal to do so deserved to be condemned, although such condemnation should probably have been directed at the United States and other major powers more than at Annan personally. They are the ones who dominate and control the UN. They have the final say on everything that is done by the UN. If they say "No," it means "No."

However, Annan's defiance in defence of the UN, especially of the United States which dominates the world body, only invited stinging attacks from Rwandan officials. As reported by *The New York Times*:

"The UN secretary-general walked into a political ambush at week's end (7 – 8 May 1998), absorbing several highly personal attacks from Rwandan leaders who blame the United Nations for failing to intervene in the 1994 genocide here.

For most of his visit, the secretary-general, Kofi Annan, defiantly defended his decisions in 1994, when he was head of peacekeeping operations, arguing that world leaders had failed to provide the UN with the troops and the mandate needed to stop the killing. 'I have no regrets,' he said.

On Friday morning, as he visited a shed full of skulls belonging to victims of the genocide in Mwurire, 50 kilometers (30 miles) outside Kigali, Mr. Annan tried again to point out that the major powers had known about the genocide, but were not willing to intervene. 'The international community could not muster the resources or the will to come to Rwanda's aid,' he told a group of survivors.

But even while he admitted that everyone had failed Rwanda, Mr. Annan resisted casting blame on specific members of the Security Council, which had the final say over sending more troops to save Tutsi victims. In essence, Mr. Annan took a political beating here to protect Western leaders who, despite receiving early warnings of the impending slaughter, resisted getting involved in the Rwandan massacres until it was far too late to help.

Put simply, Mr. Annan took the abuse to shield the United States. It was the Americans, still stinging from their failed pcacckccping operation in Somalia in 1993, who had resisted getting involved in the Rwandan killing in the spring of 1994 until it was far too late to save most of the genocide victims, aides to Mr. Annan said privately. 'The Americans said no,' one aide said. 'It was fresh after Somalia, and the Americans were not going to have it.'"[124]

Had Somalia been Britain or Germany, with a failed

91

UN peacekeeping operation intended to save lives in a major civil war, and had Belgium been Rwanda with massacres of at least 8,000 people going on everyday in a systematic campaign to exterminate an entire people, the United States and other European countries would have intervened to stop the violence and the killings. The answer is obvious as was the case with Kosovo where ethnic cleansing did not even reach the genocidal level it did in Rwanda. It is in this context that the anger of the Rwanda leaders and their people must be placed in order to understand their bitter feelings towards the United Nations and appreciate the enormity of the betrayal of this embattled African nation by the international community. As Alain Destexhe, the Belgian senator who initiated an exhaustive inquiry by a Belgian parliamentary committee into the Rwandan genocide, said about General Dallaire's cable when he testified before the United States Congress on 10 May 1998:

"How many times since 1945 has the UN received a fax from its force commander in a country warning of the likely possibility of an extermination?....

Why did the secretariat of the UN not authorize General Dallaire to go ahead with the mission of arms recovery he proposed to carry out?....

Finally, even if some key member states of the UN were reluctant to act, was it not the secretary-general's (Boutros Boutros Ghali's) role to warn the Security Council or even go public and speak about the genocide to be committed in Rwanda?

I strongly believe that if General Dallaire's cable had been published on the front page of *The New York Times* or *The Washington Post*, the genocide could have been prevented."[125]

Kofi Annan did, of course, take most of the blame – since he was in charge of UN peacekeeping operations during that period – and bore the brunt of criticism from the Rwandan leaders. But the conflict between Annan, hence the United Nations, and the Rwandan leaders also highlighted another ugly political reality in Rwanda from the time the Tutsi-dominated Rwandan Patriotic Army (RPA) stopped the genocide after sweeping across the country in 14 weeks of civil war that left the country in ruins.

It was convenient for the Tutsi-dominated government to blame the international community for failing to save Rwanda from itself. And the government had a number of reasons for keeping the memory of the UN's betrayal alive. The government was dominated by the Tutsi and was therefore discriminatory, forcing the Hutu to play a subordinate role. Also, it was determined to exact retribution for the ethnic pogroms.

And the fact that the Tutsi rebels of the Rwandan Patriotic Front stopped the massacres while the rest of the world did nothing to help gave the regime legitimacy and the moral authority to rule, although it did not have the mandate from the Hutu majority – therefore the democratic right – to do so.

Also the unwillingness by the United Nations, hence the world's major powers controlling the UN Security Council, to intervene made it hard for Western countries to criticise the Rwandan Tutsi-dominated government for its violation of human rights especially among the Hutu who became the primary target of this vindictive campaign of terror, torture and murder at the hands of Tutsi soldiers; the kind of atrocities which constituted crimes against humanity and which should have been used to indict Tutsi leaders before an international criminal tribunal.

Other countries should have been equally indicted. And that includes the United States for not only sanctioning genocide in Rwanda but for committing war crimes in Vietnam. Telford Taylor, the chief prosecutor of Nazi war criminals at the Nuremberg trials and an American himself, also advanced the same argument that the United States did indeed commit war crimes in Vietnam.[126]

Tragically, the Tutsi-dominated Rwandan government perpetrated the same kind of atrocities President Juvénal Habyarimana's Hutu regime did against the Tutsi, although on a somewhat smaller scale than the Hutu government did against the Tutsi. But the hundreds of thousands of Hutu civilian refugees in Zaire, and thousands others who perished in Rwanda at the hands of Tutsi soldiers were definitely victims of war crimes and crimes against humanity. Their plight can not be ignored or dismissed as a mere footnote to the history of the 1994 Rwandan genocide against the Tutsi.

Unfortunately, the UN and the international community in general never addressed that.

And while criticism of the United Nations continued in Rwanda, fuelled by Kofi Annan's visit to that traumatised country, the Rwandan international war crimes tribunal operating from neighbouring Tanzania handed out sentences to more convicts for their participation in the 1994 holocaust.

On 21 May 1998, Obed Ruzindana, a businessman, was sentenced to life in prison for promising Tutsis refuge in churches and at a sports stadium, then leading Hutus to kill them. And Clement Kayishema, a former governor, was also sentenced on the same day to 25 years in prison for helping Ruzindana.[127]

Although the tribunal continued to try cases, it was also plagued with a lot of problems including accusations of nepotism, misappropriation of funds, and mismanagement. But it was also struggling to operate with far fewer resources than than those given to its counterpart at The Hague that was handling war crimes perpetrated in Bosnia and other parts of the former Yugoslavia; a disparity highlighted by the tribunal's administrative officer, Agwu Ukiwe Okali: "We need investigators, administrators, bilingual lawyers, interpreters and court stenographers."[128]

Okali, a Nigerian-born graduate of the London School of Economics and Harvard Law School, took over in 1997 as registrar of the Rwandan international war crimes tribunal after UN Secretary-General Kofi Annan dismissed its senior officials. In May 1998, he went to the United Nations where he made a strong plea for help.

The Rwandan tribunal was entitled to such assistance from the UN because it was the Security Council itself – that dominates the UN – which created the court in the autumn of 1994 to handle genocide cases and other major crimes perpetrated in Rwanda earlier that year. As Okali put it: "You can't just run down the street (in Arusha, Tanzania) and buy computer parts."[129]

But despite its problems, the Rwandan tribunal had a big agenda. And it had indicted and taken into custody more people than the Balkans tribunal at The Hague did.[130]

The Rwandan tragedy will go down in history as the most tragic on the continent as a deliberate attempt to exterminate an entire people. What is even more disgusting is that it could have been prevented.

Probably more than anybody else, it was the United States which bore the biggest responsibility for what happened in Rwanda in terms of failure to provide help needed to prevent the holocaust. Had intervention taken place, all those people would not have died. Therefore there would have been no need for the International Criminal Tribunal for Rwanda (ICTR).

America's role in the Rwandan genocide continued to draw sharp criticism years after the holocaust. Some of the sharpest criticism came from one of the highest-ranking former American officials, Herman Cohen.

In July 1998, Cohen, who served as assistant secretary of state for African Affairs under President George H.W. Bush (1989 – 1992), testified before a French parliamentary committee on the 1994 Rwandan genocide and was highly critical of the American decision not to

95

intervene. He testified on July 7th before a committee investigating charges that the French intervention slowed the advance of the predominantly Tutsi Rwandan Patriotic Army (RPA) of the Rwandan Patriotic Front (RPF) from their bases in Uganda seeking to overthrow the Hutu anti-Tutsi government in Kigali which was supported by France; and that by doing so, enabled the perpetrators of the genocide to flee to what was then known as Zaire.

Cohen, who was no longer in government service when he testified, said the United States stopped the United Nations from sending 5,000 African soldiers who may have prevented the massacres in Rwanda in 1994:

"After the earlier killing of American soldiers in Somalia, I could understand there was no question of sending American troops to Africa, but I could not accept the United States opposing the sending of African troops. After all, an African farmer is not going to cut off his neighbor's head if a foreign soldier is nearby looking on."[131]

Cohen was assistant secretary of state from April 1989 to April 1993. Therefore he was not in office when the massacres began in April 1994. But he was in office during an earlier French intervention in 1990 which, he said, helped stabilise the situation and prevent an earlier catastrophe.

Since leaving office, Cohen frequently issued scathing criticism of America's refusal to intervene in Rwanda and stop the genocide. On America's support to the predominantly Tutsi rebels of the Rwandan Patriotic Army (RPA) when they were waging war against the Hutu regime in Rwanda in order to overthrow it, Cohen said:

"We provided zero support for the rebels, zero arms, zero logistics. The only support we gave was in training a dozen Tutsi officers, who were trained because they were then members of the Ugandan Army."[132]

One of those Tutsi officers was Paul Kagame who went on to become the most powerful man in the Rwandan government after the RPA seized power in July 1994. He was the chief of intelligence in the Ugandan army of President Yoweri Museveni, the Ugandan People's Defence Force (UPDF), and received military training at the United States Army Command and General Staff College in Fort Leavenworth, Kansas. Earlier, he had also received training at the Tanzania Military Academy at Monduli in Arusha Region in the northeastern part of the country. It was also in Tanzania where Kagame received some of his training as an intelligence officer.

After the genocide, the United States became increasingly close to the Tutsi-dominated government of the Rwandan Patriotic Front (RPF) and its army, the Rwandan Patriotic Army (RPA). The American government provided substantial military aid to the Rwandan army, and the United States Army Special Forces and other military personnel trained hundreds of Rwandan soldiers, most of them Tutsis:

"But Kagame and his colleagues had designs of their own. While the Green Berets trained the Rwandan Patriotic Army, that army was itself secretly training Zairian rebels. Rwandan forces then crossed into Zaire and joined with the rebels to attack refugee camps where exiled Rwandan extremists were holed up. That touched off a war that eventually toppled Africa's longest-reigning dictator, Mobutu Sese Seko of Zaire."[133]

The ouster of Mobutu had the blessings of former Tanzanian President Julius Nyerere. He wanted Mobutu out of power and supported Laurent Kabila in his plan to overthrow the Zairean dictator. Both agreed that Mobutu had to go. Nyerere met with Kabila to discuss Mobutu's ouster and how it would be accomplished.

Nyerere was not president of Tanzania during that time – he stepped down in 1985 – and therefore could not use Tanzanian resources to help overthrow Mobutu. Instead, it was agreed that troops to overthrow Mobutu would be provided by Rwanda and Uganda. Insiders, close to Nyerere during that period, said Paul Kagame and Yoweri Museveni met with Nyerere before the invasion of Zaire to discuss the matter and kept him informed of the progress after the invasion was launched.

Kagame and Museveni had great respect and admiration for Nyerere and regarded him as their mentor. And they all agreed Mobutu must go.

After Mobutu was overthrown, Nyerere visited Kabila, who was then the new leader of Congo, and was said to have been the first leader to do so, although his visit to Kinshasa was unofficial since he was no longer president of Tanzania. But he was still a regional power broker who had great influence over leaders such as Kagame and Museveni as well as others in the region.

American support for the Tutsi regime in Rwanda had domino effect in the region, which included the massacre of hundreds of thousands of Hutus in Zaire; a tragic outcome, except the ouster of Mobutu. It also strengthened the Tutsi army and security forces within Rwanda itself, thus contributing to the oppression and indiscriminate killings of Hutu civilians by what is undoubtedly a highly efficient and ruthless security apparatus with few equals on the embattled continent. And as one diplomat in Kigali described the Tutsi-dominated government, it was, in essence, a "disguised military dictatorship."[134]

The role Kagame played in the imposition of this dictatorship on the people of Rwanda, which was also a reconstituted Tutsi ethnocracy, and in the unfolding tragic drama of war and bloodshed in the Great Lakes region, can not be underestimated.

When the Tutsi-dominated Rwandan Patriotic Army

(RPA) first invaded Rwanda from Uganda in October 1990, Kagame was then a colonel in the Ugandan army and getting military training in the United States. He dropped out of military school in the United States and returned home to take command of the RPA. He later took part in the negotiations which led to a power-sharing agreement with the Hutu. The agreement, known as the Arusha Accords, was signed in Arusha, Tanzania, on 4 August 1993.

The peace agreement collapsed in April 1994, triggering the genocide; a holocaust Kagame in which himself was implicated when a secret UN report in early 2000 said he engineered the assassination of Hutu President Juvénal Habyarimana in a mysterious "accident" in which the president's plane was shot down over Kigali, sparking the genocide.

Rwanda and the entire Great Lakes region was never the same again. And that included Zaire, a very large country in the heart of Africa, where the Rwandan army came to be deeply involved in pursuit of Rwanda's national interests.

A United Nations report released in June 1998 concluded that the Rwandan army was involved in abuses during the war in Zaire – which led to the ouster of President Mobutu Sese Seko in May 1997 – that "constitute crimes against humanity" including the massacre of unarmed civilians and refugees.

That was a strong indictment backed up by evidence. Since the UN concluded that the Rwandan army, hence the Rwandan government, committed such crimes, there was no reason why Rwandan leaders – who were predominantly Tutsi – could not be prosecuted before an international criminal tribunal for atrocities which were definitely covered by the Geneva Convention under the same articles which triggered charges against their Hutu counterparts for the 1994 genocide.

Crimes against humanity by the Tutsi were no different

from crimes against humanity by the Hutu. Genocide is genocide regardless of differences in terms scale. Tragically in the case of Rwanda, the Geneva Convention was invoked selectively, sparing some culprits who happened to be members of the Tutsi clique which seized power in July 1994, ending the genocide. They should have been brought before the International Criminal Tribunal for Rwanda (ICTR) to face charges.

There is no question that the tribunal had its shortcomings in a number of areas, especially in terms of resources and lack of mandate to impose the death penalty on those who deserved the punishment for the kind of crimes they committed during the genocide. But in spite off its shortcomings, the tribunal set important precedents besides the conceptual framework for future rulings and other legal procedures of an anticipated permanent international war crimes court. Two rulings by the ICTR stand out:

"The United Nations said Jean Kambanda, the prime minister who led Rwanda's government during the1994 genocide,...was the first person ever to plead guilty to genocide charges before an international tribunal, and the judgment against...Jean-Paul Akayesu, a former Hutu mayor of the central village of Taba,...(was) the first for the crime of genocide by an international court under a 1948 (genocide) treaty. It will also be the tribunal's first verdict since it was set up in November 1994."[135]

On 4 September 1998, the International Criminal Tribunal for Rwanda, in the first genocide sentence by an international court, sentenced former Prime Minister Jean Kambanda to life in prison for his role in the 1994 genocide. He was the highest-ranking former leader of Rwanda in the tribunal's custody, and stood stoically while the three-judge panel rejected his pleas for leniency.

Many Rwandans had vivid and spine-chilling

memories of the slight man with a bushy beard, clad in fatigues, as he handed out guns and bullets as well as machetes to Hutu civilians to hunt down and kill Tutsi "cockroaches," known as *Inyenzi* in Kinyarwanda, the language spoken in Rwanda.

The tribunal's chief judge, Laity Kama of Senegal, reading the judgement, said his crimes "carry an intrinsic gravity, and their widespread atrocious and systematic character is particularly shocking to the human conscience."[136]

But many Rwandans were outraged when they heard the judgement. As Alice Karekezi, a Tutsi who lost many friends in the slaughter, said: "Life in prison, so what? That won't bring back the dead....I was remembering him as a warrior...seeing him like that (in a somber suit and tie that replaced the military garb) was strange."[137]

Karekezi was one of the Rwandans who attended the genocide trials in Arusha, Tanzania.

Kambanda, 42, had pleaded guilty in May 1998. Although his sentencing was the first for the crime of genocide by an international court, the tribunal's first conviction of genocide came on 2 September 1998 against former village mayor Jean-Paul Akayesu. And unlike Kambanda, all the Nazi war defendants at the Nuremberg trials pleaded not guilty to the charges brought against them, including murder and extermination.

Defence lawyer Nicholas Taingaye seemed to try to maintain the integrity of the court when he said in his closing argument in March 1998 in the trial of Akayesu – which began on 9 January 1997 – that the former teacher and mayor should be acquitted of charges he ordered the massacre of 2,000 people because "a wrongful conviction would lend credence to the tribunal's detractors."[138]

But prosecutor Pierre Prosper countered that Akayesu, born in 1953, knew of crimes against the Tutsi, "and at times, was present during their commission, but failed to prevent them, and actually aided and abetted their commission."[139]

The verdict against Akayesu was not only the first by an international tribunal in the 1994 holocaust; it was also the first judgement by an international court on the crime of genocide, and the first in Africa involving war crimes committed on African soil.

In the case of Kambanda who pleaded guilty on 1 May 1998, the former prime minister promised to testify against other alleged ringleaders of the genocide, unlike Akayesu who denied all the charges brought against him. But Kambanda's willingness to cooperate with the prosecution did not win him any leniency, and he was given the maximum sentence of life in prison.

UN Secretary-General Kofi Annan said in New York: "The success of this court in prosecuting genocide is a historic and defining example of the ability of the United Nations to create institutions which fulfill the highest aspirations of mankind."[140]

When the tribunal secured the convictions, it was also the first time an international court ruled on sexual violence. The indictment against Akayesu included rape charges. As Faiza Jama Mohammed, Africa's director of Equality Now, a New York-based organisation focusing on women's rights, said before Akayesu was convicted: "If Akayesu is convicted on the rape charges which have been brought against him, his case will represent the first successful prosecution of sexual violence by an international tribunal."[141] He was convicted on 9 of 15 counts ranging from genocide to torture and rape.

Annan hailed the verdict as a major advance in international human rights law. He said the court's decision would send a powerful message to violators of human rights around the world that they can no longer target ethnic minorities with impunity, although only abuses covered by the 1948 Genocide Convention adjudicated in an international context would be dealt with.

Speaking from South Africa where he was attending a

102

summit of the Nonaligned Movement of Third World countries in Durban, Annan said: "This judgment is a testament to our collective determination to confront the heinous crime of genocide in a way we never have before. Let us never again be accused of standing while genocide and crimes against humanity are being commited."[142] The verdict against Akayesu also set legal precedent by establishing the crime of rape as an act of genocide as interpreted under the 1948 Genocide Convention.

Several witnesses including four female victims testified that Akayesu permitted the rape of Tutsi women in his town hall office. As Binaifer Nowrogee, a specialist on sexual war crimes at Human Rights Watch, explained, thousands of Tutsi women were raped: "He himself did not commit the rape. But he was in a position to prevent or punish those who did. But he did nothing."[143]

Other war crimes tribunals, including the Nuremberg and Tokyo war crimes tribunals established after World War II to prosecute German and Japanese defendants, handed down convictions for committing a variety of war crimes including rape. And the Bosnia war crimes court for the former Yugoslavia at The Hague indicted several people for genocide, including former Bosnian leaders Ratko Mladic and Radovan Karadzic.

But the verdict against Akayesu on 2 September 1998 represented the first time that an international war crimes tribunal had found a person guilty of committing genocide which is defined by the Genocide Convention as seeking to kill or harm members of an ethnic, racial, religious or national group with "the intent to destroy in whole or in part."

In an attempt to clear himself of the charges brought against him, Akayesu employed a defence reminiscent of the argument advanced by German war criminals during World War II, contending before the tribunal in March 1998 that he could not resist "the force of evil which grew everywhere."[144] But he could not sway the court.

In Rwanda, the verdict against Akayesu did not impress many people, especially the Tutsi. It was seen as mild compared with the death penalty imposed on 22 defendants who were publicly executed on 24 April 1998 to the applause of thousands of people who witnessed the executions. As Patrick Mazimhaka, a senior Rwandan official, said about the verdict: "I don't see the people in Rwanda going to the streets to congratulate the international court on this one."[145] The implication was obvious: Akayesu deserved the death penalty.

The reaction to Jean Kambanda's trial was the same. His defence lawyer, Michael Inglis, said on 3 September 1998 that the former prime minister was a mere puppet used by a powerful military during the 1994 genocide. "The strings were pulled and he danced."[146]

Rwandans sitting in the gallery of the international court in Arusha, Tanzania, laughed in derision as the lawyer pleaded for a two-year sentence or none at all for his client, contending that such leniency was necessary "to enable the healing to take place."[147] Prosecutors refuted the argument and went on to say that Kambanda deserved life imprisonment even though he had pleaded guilty to genocide and promised to testify against other killers.

Although Akayesu pleaded not guilty, he asked for forgiveness from his fellow countrymen. But the court was not impressed by his plea for forgiveness as a mitigating factor in his sentencing. On 2 October 1998, the UN tribunal sentenced him to life in prison for his role in the deaths of 2,000 people who had sought his protection.

Akayesu, who portrayed himself as a simple mayor of a small town powerless to stop the ethnic violence, also was sentenced to 80 years for other war crimes including rape. In the first judgement by an international court, Akayesu was convicted on 2 September 1998 of nine counts in connection with the massacre of Tutsis and moderate Hutus.

Judge Laity Kama, who was also the president of the

international war crimes tribunal, ruled that Akayesu "chose to participate in the genocide" and should spend the rest of his life in prison.[148] The presiding judge went on to say: "The chamber is of the opinion...that genocide constitutes the crime of crimes."[149] Akayesu was ordered to serve the sentences for genocide, crimes against humanity and other violations concurrently, which meant he would serve a single life sentence.

Before his sentencing on 2 October, Akayesu had made an impassioned plea on 28 September for forgiveness from his fellow Rwandans for his failure – critics said his refusal – to stop the killings by Hutu extremists wielding machetes and nail-studded clubs. The court acknowledged that Akayesu initially prevented the massacres in the central village of Taba, where he served as mayor, and played a small role in the government that orchestrated the genocidal campaign. But Judge Kama ruled that Akayesu later endorsed the plan to exterminate Tutsis throughout the country and was "individually and criminally responsible for the deaths."[150]

The life sentence was the maximum the court could impose under its UN mandate even for the most heinous crimes, but survivors of the holocaust and Rwandan government officials wished he had been tried in Rwanda where he definitely would have been sentenced to death.

The enormity of Akayesu's crimes was underscored by the prosecutors who said that although the former Rwandan mayor was sentenced to three life terms in prison, to be served concurrently, the punishment was still not severe enough. And as Judge Kama put it: "(The crimes) particularly shock the collective conscience."[151]

Akayesu was given life terms for genocide, incitement to commit genocide, and crimes against humanity relating to extermination. The Judge also sentenced him to 15 years each on four separate counts of crimes against humanity related to murder and rape and 10 years for separate counts of crimes against humanity related to torture and other inhuman acts.[152]

The rulings against Akayesu and Kambanda constituted a precedent whose significance was noted by Kingsley Chiedu Moghalu, legal adviser to the International Criminal Tribunal for Rwanda (ICTR), in his article "Rwanda Panel's Legacy: They Can Run But Not Hide":

"Responsible members of the international community will not forget crimes against humanity committed by political rulers, but will seek ways to punish them and thus deter such future crimes....The most important precedent-setting case of this kind has emerged from a United Nations tribunal in Africa that has struck the most effective judicial blow against impunity to date....

Mr. Kambanda had pleaded guilty to...genocide and crimes against humanity..., essentially admitting (in his capacity as Rwanda's prime minister during the 1994 genocide) that the criminal enterprise of Rwanda's mass killings was a state-sponsored plan aimed at wiping out the country's Tutsi ethnic minority. This judgment was a landmark in international law.

In the years after World War I, several unsuccessful attempts were made to establish international tribunals to prosecute individuals responsible for war crimes. But the international criminal justice took root only after World War II with the tribunals set up by the Allied powers in Nuremberg and Tokyo to prosecute German and Japanese war criminals. It was not until 1948 that the UN General Assembly adopted the Genocide Convention, a treaty requiring the signatory countries to prevent and punish genocide....

The trials at the Rwanda tribunal in Arusha are especially important for Africa because the court is adjudicating crimes committed in a civil war that was similar to many others in the continent. The Arusha tribunal's work tells Africans that there is hope for redress of crimes against humanity, and sends a message to the leaders and warlords on the continent who are retarding its political evolution, economic development and social cohesion. It is planting a seed which...should give potential perpetrators of genocide reason to rethink before they act....Those who commit serious crimes against humanity may try to run, but they can no longer hide."[153]

Probably the best way for Africa to deal with these war criminals and other notorious abusers of human rights, including presidents many of whom routinely abuse their power and even sanction extra-judicial killings, is by establishing its own continental tribunal under the auspices of the Organisation of Unity (OAU) – after it has been radically transformed into an efficient functional apparatus – similar to the European high court instituted by the European Union; empower the continental criminal court to impose stiff sentences including the death penalty; extradite offenders who have sought refuge in other African countries – if their hosts are unwilling or refuse to extradite them, bounty hunters should be offered an irresistible financial inducement to capture them and bring them before the continental tribunal; and ask the international community to apprehend African criminals who have sought refuge or who are hiding outside Africa and extradite them to stand trial before the continental criminal court based in Addis Ababa, Africa's political capital and OAU headquarters, or in any other African country where African governments, human rights and non-governmental organisations agree to establish the tribunal.

Also, all countries, African and non-African, should have universal jurisdiction they can invoke to apprehend, try and convict anybody, from any country, who has committed crimes against humanity.

But, first and foremost, responsibility for dealing with African offenders should be Africa's. However, given the despicable record of most African leaders notorious for dictatorship, and who have virtually sworn to protect each other, it is going to be extremely difficult to establish a continental criminal court of functional utility.

Unless appropriate measures are taken with the help of the international community to make it functional – it is a such a shame that we Africans have to depend so much on other people to get things done – the African High Court could end up being as weak and as useless as the Organisation of African Unity (OAU), which is no more than a prestigious debating club, because of the conspiratorial silence of most African leaders that is so deafening when human rights are being violated in their own countries; a betrayal of African aspirations which prompted Julius Nyerere in the late 1970s to dismiss the OAU as "a trade union of tyrants."

However, the success of the International Criminal Tribunal for Rwanda in prosecuting some of the genocide suspects was cause for optimism on a continent that has earned more than its share of stereotypes: "Nothing good comes out of Africa." Except gold and diamonds, of course, among other resources including oil.

Not long after the trial of Jean-Paul Akayesu and Jean Kambanda ended, another genocide suspect was convicted by the war crimes tribunal in Arusha, Tanzania. On 14 December 1998, Omar Serushago, a leader of the notorious Interahamwe militia in the Hutu traditional stronghold of Gisenyi province in northwestern Rwanda, became the second defendant – after Kambanda (Akayesu maintained his innocence throughout his trial) – to plead guilty to charges of genocide and other crimes perpetrated during the 1994 holocaust.

Serushago, 37, pleaded guilty to one count of genocide and three counts against humanity related to murder, extermination and torture. A fifth count of crimes against humanity involving rape, to which he pleaded not guilty, was dropped. The indictment against Serushago provided details on his role in the massacres and described one incident in which Hutu soldiers and militiamen abducted about 20 Tutsis who had sought refuge in Gisenyi: "They took them to a place known as 'Commune Rouge' and executed them. Omar Serushago personally killed four of the 20 persons."[154]

As the trials went on in Tanzania, the pursuit of other genocide suspects also continued in other countries. On 19 February 1999, Kenyan authorities arrested Casimir Bizimungu who served as health minister in the interim Rwandan government formed after the 1994 genocide. The former Rwandan information minister, Eliezer Niyitegeka, was also arrested, bringing to 12 the number of suspects held in Kenya for handing over to the international war crimes tribunal.[155]

But in a controversial decision in March 1999 that may have impaired the court's credibility, the tribunal freed a former Rwandan major, Bernard Ntuyahaga, accused of murdering 10 Belgian UN-peacekeeping soldiers during the genocide. Prosecutors dropped the charges after Belgian authorities sought his transfer to Belgium so that he could stand trial trial there for the murders. The court ruled that it had no jurisdiction to hand him over to the Belgian government to be prosecuted.[156]

The release of Ntuyahaga triggered protests from Belgium and Rwanda. When prosecutors dropped the charges against him, they believed that he could be handed over to the Belgian authorities. But the plan backfired when the International Criminal Tribunal for Rwanda (ICTR) said it had no power to "hand over someone to any government,"[157] obviously because of its limited mandate prescribed by the UN Security Council when the Council established the tribunal in November 1994.

But soon after Ntuyahaga was released, he was arrested by the Tanzanian authorities. A Tanzanian official said on 30 March 1999 that Ntuyahaga, wanted by both Belgium and Rwanda for his alleged role in the 1994 genocide, had been arrested, thus paving the way for his extradition.[158] He was sought by Rwandan authorities in the assassination of Prime Minister Agathe Uwilingiyimana during the frenzy of killings in April 1994.[159] He could have been extradited to either country, Belgium or Rwanda, to stand trial, although he would have preferred not to be sent back to Rwanda at all where he probably would have been sentenced to death by firing squad.

The arrest of Ntuyahaga by the Tanzanian authorities was followed a week later by the arrest of three former Rwandan cabinet members implicated in the 1994 massacres. The international war crimes tribunal announced on 7 April 1999 that the three former cabinet members were arrested in Cameroon.

The suspects were former Foreign Minister Jerome Bicamumpaka; former Commerce Minister Justin Mugenzi; and Prosper Mugiraneza who was the head of Rwanda's civil service.[160]

The prosecution of the genocide suspects went a step further, beyond Africa, when a former mayor in Rwanda went on trial before a military tribunal in April 1999 in Lausanne, Switzerland, charged with crimes relating to the massacre of Tutsis and their Hutu sympathizers in 1994. The trial of Fulgence Ntiyonteze, 35, was the first of a Rwandan war crimes suspect in a Western country. Ntiyonteze went to Switzerland in 1994 and was arrested in 1996.[161] His prosecution by the Swiss authorities also gave some hope to the survivors of the genocide that some members of the international community were doing at least something to pursue justice against the perpetrators of the holocaust.

Ntiyonteze's prosecution was, about a month later, followed by the conviction of Dr. Clement Kayishema, a 45-year-old former provincial governor, and Obed Ruzindana, a 37-year-old businessman, by the war crimes tribunal. Both were found guilty of genocide: "Dr. Kayishema – who was accused of promising Tutsis refuge in churches and at a sports stadium, then leading them to death – was given four life sentences. Mr. Ruzindana, accused of aiding Mr. Kayishema, was sentenced to 25 years in prison."[162]

However, the succession of the judicial proceedings – the trial in Switzerland followed by the two convictions of Kayishema and Ruzindana in Tanzania – was probably coincidental, although it may also have given the impression that dispensation of justice was going on fairly well; even if it was slow, and the maximum life sentence, mandated by the UN Security Council, was not severe enough for the perpetrators of the genocide convicted by the war crimes tribunal in Tanzania.

Another encouraging sign was that the former Rwandan cabinet members who were arrested in Kenya and Cameroon were among the nine former ministers in the Hutu genocidal regime awaiting trial,[163] in addition to former Prime Minister Kambanda who had already been convicted. There was even talk of extending the tribunal's mandate to cover crimes against humanity committed elsewhere on the African continent: in Burundi, Sierra Leone, Mozambique, and Angola.

Those were the countries named, but that is not the whole list.

Several others should have been added to the list. Other prime candidates for prosecution include war criminals and perpetrators of crimes against humanity in Liberia, former warlord and later president, Charles Taylor, being one of them; Somalia, Uganda, Congo-Kinshasa, Congo-Brazzaville, Chad, Ethiopia, especially during dictator Mengistu Haile Mariam's reign of terror; as well as Sudan and Mauritania notorious for enslaving and killing blacks; and Rwanda itself where crimes against humanity have also been committed by the victorious Rwandan Patriotic Front (RPF) and its army, the Rwandan Patriotic Army (RPA), against Hutu civilians including those who fled to Congo for refuge, and not just those committed by the Hutu perpetrators of the genocide who also continued to commit crimes against humanity, especially from their sanctuary in eastern Congo, targeting Tutsis in Rwanda.

Unfortunately in all those countries, the people notorious for perpetrating diabolical iniquities against their fellow countrymen and others – including missionaries and relief workers from different parts of the world – were either in power (Charles Taylor in Liberia and his alter ego and protégé Foday Sankoh in Sierra Leone are perfect examples), too powerful to be arrested let alone be prosecuted, or were brought – in some cases such as Sierra Leone, they forced their way – into the government as part of an effort to end civil wars; a compromise that virtually guaranteed them immunity from prosecution.

However, the international war crimes tribunal in Arusha, Tanzania, lost whatever little credibility it had with the Rwandan officials when it dropped its case against Jean-Bosco Barayagwiza.

Joseph Mutaboba, the Rwandan representative to the United Nations, described the 49-year-old Barayagwiza as the "Number 1" criminal wanted for fomenting genocide. He also denounced the International Criminal Tribunal for Rwanda (ICTR), saying it was neglecting its duties.

The release of Barayagwiza ignited such a storm of protest from Rwandan officials, who temporarily suspended cooperation with the tribunal on other cases, because of the key role he played in the extermination campaign and was described as one of the most prominent suspects in the torture and massacre of Tutsis.

Barayagwiza was the spokesman for Rwanda's minister of foreign affairs in the Hutu government which led the genocidal campaign against the Tutsi. He also led the Coalition for the Defence of the Republic, a Hutu political party that espoused the doctrine of Hutu supremacy and hatred against the Tutsi minority. He was the mastermind of the genocide propaganda. And he helped start the notorious and virulently anti-Tutsi Radio Television Libres des Milles Collines which incited Hutus to exterminate Tutsis.

On 3 November 1999, the Appeals Chamber of the International Criminal Tribunal for Rwanda decided that Barayagwiza must be released because his fundamental rights had been violated by prolonged detention without trial. The appeals panel of judges based at The Hague in the Netherlands went on to say that the tribunal's prosecutor, Canadian jurist Louise Arbor, had not informed Barayagwiza of the charges against him and had not transferred him quickly enough from prison in Cameroon where he was arrested on 27 March 1996 and detained for 19 months before being handed over to the tribunal in Arusha, Tanzania.

Barayagwiza was accused of genocide, incitement of genocide and crimes against humanity which guaranteed him life imprisonment if he were to be convicted. Mutaboba described him as "one of the architects" of the holocaust and added: "The hardship he allegedly suffered in Cameroon jails is negligible compared to the suffering his victims endured."[164]

Mutaboba also said the dismissal of the case against Barayagwiza created "a terrible precedent" that other genocide defendants could use to have their cases dismissed.

Dismissing cases on simple technicalities and other procedural grounds was not unprecedented in judicial proceedings around the world but would have impaired the credibility of the war crimes tribunal even among some of its most ardent supporters.

By November 1999, at least 3 of the 38 defendants awaiting trial contested their imprisonment on the same grounds as Barayagwiza. As Zephyr Mutanguha, Rwanda's official representative at the war crimes tribunal in Arusha, said about Barayagwiza's release: "We feel that this has set a very unfortunate precedent. The others are of course going to claim release on the same grounds. And the whole process of justice will look a mockery."[165]

After the appeal's court ordered Barayagwiza's release, he remained in jail in Tanzania and applied for extradition back to Cameroon where the court said he should be returned.[166]

The war crimes tribunal enhanced its credibility – and even regained what it had lost, at least some of it – when it continued to prosecute genocide suspects. On 6 December 1999, it convicted former militia leader Georges Rutaganda of genocide and sentenced him to life in prison. Rutaganda was vice president of the ferocious Interahamwe militia which, together with the army and security forces, spearheaded the massacre of Tutsis and moderate Hutus.[167] Judge Laity Kama said the militia leader had not shown "the slightest remorse."[168] Rutaganda was the sixth person to be convicted of genocide and the fourth to be sentenced to life in prison.

But it was the case of Jean-Bosco Barayagwiza which continued to draw attention to the tribunal's judicial proceedings and to what many perceived to be its bad judgement when it released him from custody on a legal technicality. Even one of the court's judges, Navanethem Pillay, conceded that the furor over the decision by the appeal's judges in the Netherlands to release Barayagwiza was a bad sign of what was yet to come. There is no question that the dismissal of the case reflected badly on the tribunal's integrity. As she put it: "We are in a crisis. We really have to worry what is the future of this tribunal."[169]

Probably the only consolation was that the war crimes tribunal in Tanzania, subordinate to the appeals panel at The Hague (which was part of the Bosnia tribunal for the former Yugoslavia, the senior of the two courts), was not the one that dismissed the case.

The court faced a difficult choice: " Either prosecute suspects as harshly as Rwanda wants and risk its judicial integrity, as the appeals court judges see it, or worry strictly about legal issues and risk having Rwanda cut off its help permanently. While unlikely, that move would mean an end to the tribunal, experts say."[170]

The Rwandan government itself indicated that it was not ready to sever ties with the court permanently. As the Rwandan representative to the United Nations, Joseph Mutaboba, said in denying a permanent rupture with the tribunal: "We have not burned any bridges between us and the United Nations at all."[171]

But the tribunal lost some credibility even if its integrity was not permanently impaired.

Barayagwiza's case also raised serious questions about the tribunal's independence and underscored a conflict between justice and the harsh realities of pursuing war criminals who committed atrocities in the highly volatile context of Rwanda in 1994. Although there was much sympathy for Rwanda's outrage over Barayagwiza's release, Rwandan officials undoubtedly had a hidden agenda, clumsily camouflaged – as a quest for justice – by their impassioned rhetoric demanding full prosecution of Barayagwiza.

They knew that they had committed atrocities themselves during the civil war they waged to seize power in 1994 when they were rebels of the Rwandan Patriotic Front (RPF). They also knew that they had perpetrated other atrocities and crimes against humanity after they seized power and went on to massacre at least 200,000 Hutu refugees in Zaire and thousands more within Rwanda itself, especially between 1995 and 1998; and continued to kill Hutus indiscriminately thereafter, ostensibly to neutralise Hutu rebels who were waging war against the Tutsi-dominated regime. Human Rights Watch estimated that Tutsi rebels killed at least 30,000 Hutus, mostly civilians, in Rwanda alone during their takeover of the country in 1994.

Therefore the Tutsi rulers wanted to demonstrate

whatever power and influence they had over the war crimes tribunal. They also wanted to divert attention from the atrocities they had committed in order to avoid investigation and prosecution for their crimes under the same Genocide Convention that was being used against their enemies. Barayagwiza's case gave them the perfect opportunity to do that. They used it to impugn the integrity of the international war crimes tribunal, while claiming moral high ground for stopping the 1994 genocide against the Tutsi and Hutu moderates, knowing full well that they themselves had also committed some of the worst atrocities against the Hutu which not only amounted to genocide but helped perpetuate the conflict and destabilise the entire Great Lakes region of East-central Africa.

The appeals court itself at The Hague helped to discredit the Rwandan war crimes tribunal and even bolstered, however indirectly, the Tutsi regime's position – which Rwandan officials claimed was no more than a quest for justice – when the judges wrote:

"Nothing less than the integrity of the tribunal is at stake in this case. Loss of public confidence in the tribunal, as a court valuing human rights of all individuals – including those charged with unthinkable crimes – would be among the most serious consequences of allowing the appellant to stand trial in the face of such violations of his rights."[172]

The Tutsi-dominated Rwandan government was outraged by the appeals court ruling and immediately suspended cooperation with the war crimes tribunal in Tanzania.

The suspension was a blow to the judicial proceedings in Tanzania because almost every witness who had to testify before the war crimes tribunal had to travel from Rwanda to Tanzania, and the tribunal's investigators had to go to Rwanda to talk to potential witnesses to gather evidence against the defendants. Without Rwanda's cooperation and permission, nothing could be done. No more witnesses would be able to go to Tanzania. And the tribunal's investigators would no longer be allowed into Rwanda to talk to the people who witnessed the massacres and collect evidence needed to prosecute cases before the international tribunal; a court that was not even respected by the Rwandan authorities in the first place because of its perceived leniency towards genocide defendants and its inability to impose the death penalty.

Rwandan officials insisted that Barayagwiza, who was still being held in Tanzania after the appeals judges in the Netherlands ordered that he must be released, was a prominent holocaust leader; he played a critical role in the genocide and must face his day in court regardless of the 19-month detention he was subjected to – even before he was charged with anything – and which the judges found to be excessive and unjust.

The war crimes tribunal prosecutors in Tanzania argued that the court was not to blame because Barayagwiza was detained in Cameroon at Rwanda's request, not theirs. But Rwandan officials dismissed the injustice he suffered – by being detained for so long without any formal charges being brought against him – as minor and irrelevant compared to the monumental suffering and loss of hundreds of thousands of lives during the 1994 genocide for which he was largely responsible. As Richard Sezibera, Rwanda's ambassador to the United States, said:

"If one would weigh the potential injustice to one man against the injustice to millions of people, a strictly legal interpretation of the issues would not be one to make. If one wanted to make a comparison – that is not explicitly accurate but indicative – it would be like releasing Goebbels of Nazi Germany on a technicality. And that is not acceptable. It should not be acceptable to the world."[173]

It was also clear why Rwandan officials felt Barayagwiza's release would set a dangerous precedent. Four other defendants filed motions for release on similar grounds. They included probably the most notorious and sought-after suspect, Colonel Theoneste Bagosora, who organised the genocide, opened the armoury and handed out weapons to Hutu militia gangs to massacre Tutsis.

But despite its legitimate concern for justice, hence the demand that Barayagwiza must be punished, the Rwandan government was not in a position to cut off ties with the UN war crimes tribunal permanently. If it did that, it would have to spend its meagre resources finding the perpetrators of the genocide and having them extradited from different countries, some of which would be unwilling to send them back to Rwanda where they would most likely be executed; unlike in Tanzania where they would be sentenced to life in prison if convicted of the most serious crimes, since the tribunal did not have the mandate to impose the death penalty and was therefore the better court for the genocide defendants.

And even if all the suspects – covered by the Genocide Convention, hence subject to prosecution by the international war crimes tribunal in Tanzania – were to be rounded up by the Rwandan authorities, the country's overburdened courts would not be able to handle all those cases; at least not according to internationally accepted norms of justice. Rwanda's prisons were already packed with more than 130,000 suspects, an enormous burden that would take years to clear even for the country's judicial system notorious for dispensing kangaroo justice.

The international war crimes tribunal adhered to higher standards as happened in Barayagwiza's case. "At the heart of the case lie thorny questions about international criminal justice. How much should the tribunal be made accountable to the people of Rwanda, and how much should it strive to fulfill the highest standards of international law?"[174]

While the appeals court of the international war crimes tribunal was reconsidering its decision to set Barayagwiza free (he was still in custody in Tanzania), another prominent genocide suspect who had been free for years was sent back to Africa to stand trial in Tanzania for his role in the massacre of Tutsis. In March 2000, Elizaphan Ntakirutimana, a 75-year-old Seventh-day Adventist minister, was extradited to Tanzania from the United States where he fled after the 1994 genocide in which he played a central role in his capacity as a pastor who was trusted by his Tutsi church members who desperately sought help from him when they were in danger of being killed by Hutu militia gangs.

His extradition was part of an effort, however halfheartedly, by the United States to salvage its conscience after its willful neglect of the Rwandan victims during the 1994 genocide. According to a report by *Newsweek*:

"It took almost five years and a signature last week from Secretary of State Madeleine Albright. But the United States will now send a retired Rwandan pastor back to Africa to stand trial for genocide – the first time an indicted criminal living in America has been extradited to an international court. Elizaphan Ntakirutimana, 75, a former Seventh-day Adventist preacher, has exhausted all his appeals and U.S. marshals are preparing to escort him to the United Nations International Criminal Tribunal in Tanzania, where he faces charges of genocide and crimes against humanity for the 1994 massacres in Rwanda.

Ntakirutimana, a Hutu pastor in western Rwanda, allegedly gathered thousands of Tutsis into a church compound with promises of protection, then commandeered a convoy of soldiers and militia to murder them. He fled Rwanda in July '94 at the end of the war, and made his way to Laredo, Texas, after a son, who is a prominent doctor there, helped him secure a visa. In 1996, the U.N. Tribunal indicted him. Texas authorities arrested him, and put him in a Laredo jail as his case wound through the U.S. Courts.

State Department officials said they were pleased by Ntakirutimana's extradition. They hope the case has set a legal precedent that will make the process smoother in similar situations. Ntakirutimana maintains that he is not guilty. He will be tried along with another son also charged in the massacre. If convicted, he faces life in prison."[175]

The international community itself as a whole was strongly criticized by the genocide survivors and others for its unwillingness to respond to desperate pleas for help when the Rwandan tragedy began to unfold. But it was the world's major powers, especially the United States, that came under heavy criticism for their failure to do so.

In a report released by an international panel of experts who investigated the international response – or lack thereof – to the Rwandan tragedy, UN officials and the world's major countries were blamed more than anybody else for their unwillingness to prevent or stop the holocaust. Secretary-General Kofi Annan and his predecessor, Boutros-Boutros Ghali, were among those who were blamed for the genocide. In a statement on 16 December 1999, Annan said: "On behalf of the United Nations, I acknowledge this failure and express my deep remorse."[176]

Former Swedish Prime Minister Ingvar Carlsson, who led the investigation, said at a news conference that it was "hard to understand" why the Security Council drastically reduced the UN peacekeeping force in Rwanda from 2,500 to only a few hundred when the genocide began and then increased it to 5,500 when the holocaust had run its course.

The UN's most powerful member, the United States,

did not provide any help or documents to the investigating panel during its six-month investigation and effectively blocked the Security Council in 1993 and 1994 from taking any serious action in Rwanda. And that included blocking African troops – under UN auspices – from intervening in the war-torn country to stop the genocide. In pointed reference to the United States and other major powers, Carlsson said the blame must be shouldered by "those who didn't care at all, who said Rwanda is a distant African country."[177]

The panel had three members. They were all appointed by Annan. Besides Carlsson, the other members were Han Sung-Joo, a former South Korean minister of foreign affairs and one of the country's leading scholars of international affairs; and Rufus M. Kupolati, a retired lieutenant-general from Nigeria who had played a prominent role in UN peacekeeping operations in the past in different parts of the world.

The report showed a pattern of ignored warnings and missed signals of an impending catastrophe which turned out to be one of the bloodiest holocausts in history. Pleas for help and immediate intervention from the commander of the UN-peacekeeping forces in Rwanda, General Romeo Dallaire, were simply ignored in spite of the fact that he warned UN headquarters of plans by the Hutu to exterminate the Tutsi. As the panel put it: "Information received by a United Nations mission that plans are being made to exterminate any group requires an immediate and determined response."[178]

The investigating team concluded that the instructions from the UN headquarters in New York not to seize weapons "certainly gave the signal to Interahamwe and other extremists that UNAMIR (U.N. Assistance Mission for Rwanda, the acronym for the peacekeeping force) was not going to take assertive action to deal with such caches."[179] The panel also noted that various reports in the year before the genocide had provided early warning signals of the ethnic dimensions of the ongoing civil war which started in October 1990 when the Tutsi invaded Rwanda from Uganda for the first time; ample time for the international community to have intervened or to have prepared for an intervention. Yet nothing was done.

Shortly after a power-sharing agreement was signed in Arusha, Tanzania, in August 1993 by the Hutu-led government and the Tutsi-led armed opposition (the Rwandan Patriotic Front – RPF), a joint delegation of the two parties to the conflict went to the United Nations in New York and warned that the peace accord could fall apart if it did not have strong backing. The delegation also asked for more than 4,000 UN peacekeeping troops to oversee implementation of the peace process.

Weeks later, UN Secretary-General Boutros Ghali recommended a force about half that size. But it was cut back even further by the Security Council which had no interest in Rwanda. "General Dallaire, aware of the ethnic volatility in Rwanda, proposed rules of engagement for his troops – which the investigation found were often ill-trained and ill-equipped soldiers – that would allow them to intervene in crimes against humanity. United Nations headquarters never responded to his request for approval."[180]

On 11 January 1994, about three months before the massacres started, General Dallaire sent a cable to the UN warning of impending carnage. It was this telegram that became the catalyst for charges that the United Nations and the world's major powers knew of the coming holocaust but did nothing to prevent it. As *The New York Times* stated, it was "the United States which set Mr. Annan's agenda. Washington...blocked effective UN action in Rwanda."[181] And as *The Economist* commented:

"When terrible atrocities are being carried out, or are about to be, the UN must not maintain its habitual neutrality....Neutrality may be fine when UN members are exercised about border disputes, but not when one side starts the mass obliteration of the other. Then it is time to take sides....(And) the UN – whether Secretariat or Security Council – should not threaten the use of force unless it is prepared, if necessary, to use it. Unfortunately, the UN operation in Rwanda relied, like many others, on a threat of force that the Security Council was not prepared to endorse.

In December 1993, the UN had mandated some 2,500 UN troops to monitor a peace agreement drawn up by Rwanda's Hutu-dominated government and the mostly Tutsi rebels, and to 'contribute to the security' of the country's capital, Kigali. When the civil was turned into the one-sided extermination of Tutsi civilians, the UN's bluff was called. First, the Security Council cut the peacekeeping force. Then, when the killing was nearly complete, it gave France permission to intervene with a much stronger mandate than the one it had given its own peacekeepers. This took months to get into place, because of foot-dragging by UN members, particularly the United States.

In retrospect, this seems at best like incompetence, at worst like callous indifference. But the crucial failure of political will was not the fault of UN officials. The Rwandans were let down most of all by the permanent members of the Security Council – and not, for once, China and Russia, but America, Britain and France....

And what would happen were another genocide to break out in some remote corner of the world tomorrow? A paradox of the end of the cold war is that, though the countries on the Security Council are now unconstrained by the fear of starting a nuclear exchange between the superpowers, they have little political interest in intervening in a country like Rwanda, which is of no economic value or strategic importance but brimming with practical dangers.

If outsiders are to intervene to stop such butchery in

such places in future, it will almost certainly be for humanitarian motives."[182]

Unfortunately, humanitarian concerns in other parts of the world are not a prime factor in the calculus of the economic, geopolitical and strategic interests of the major powers unless such interventions help them achieve their national goals in a global context – even emergency food assistance is sometimes an effective instrument of foreign policy – and affect people they easily identify with.

That is why President Bill Clinton did nothing, in terms of military assistance involving American troops, to help the people of Sierra Leone when they were being brutalized – massacred, and having their limbs chopped off – by the rebels of the Revolutionary United Front (who were armed and financed by Liberia, Ivory Coast and Burkina Faso), despite his earlier pledge during his visit to Rwanda that he and other world leaders would never allow such a tragedy to happen again. As he stated in Rwanda: "We did not do as much as we could have and should have."

It seems that no one, except the victims of genocide and other atrocities, learned anything from the Rwandan holocaust and other tragedies in other parts of the world including Sierra Leone. And the victims know that they can not count on the international community to rush to their rescue. As *The Washington Post* stated concerning the world's indifference to the concentrated slaughter in Rwanda:

"The shame of Rwanda is that the United Nations did send a token force to the region, as a salve to its members' consciences, but then stood by as the horror unfolded.

If the world's leading governments are indifferent to genocide, the United Nations should not act as a vehicle for token interventions to hide their shame. It should use that shame to fight indifference; it should broadcast the horror of genocide to voters and stir the outrage that might produce serious intervention. Mr. Annan likes to say that the United Nations should not be neutral in the face of evil. Indifference to evil is not a matter for polite neutrality, either."[183]

The observation by *The Washington Post*, like those of other newspapers and magazines including *The New York Times* and *The Economist* cited here, came after the release of the report by the independent panel of experts who investigated the UN's role in the Rwandan genocide. The report underscored the importance of the International Criminal Tribunal for Rwanda (ICTR) which was established in part to make amends for the UN's failure in that beleaguered nation and to salvage the conscience of those who could and *should* have prevented or stopped the holocaust. And the tribunal made a commendable effort to administer justice and may be even to help prevent future tragedies similar to the one that took place in Rwanda.

Despite its shortcomings and limited mandate, the International Criminal Tribunal for Rwanda accomplished several things: It punished some of the leading perpetrators of the 1994 genocide; it set important legal precedents; it sent a clear message to war criminals and other violators of human rights across the African continent that they can not always commit atrocities against defenceless civilians without being punished; and, by conducting judicial proceedings which entailed recounting some of the most vivid and graphic details of the Rwandan holocaust – sometimes witnesses, judges and prosecutors had to interrupt the proceedings to take a break, shedding tears – the war crimes tribunal delivered a searing indictment, however indirectly, against the international community for its failure and unwillingness to intervene in Rwanda and stop the massacres, a horrendous tragedy that may have jolted even some of the most hardened souls.

But the tribunal did not, and could not, address the fundamental issue that is at the heart of the ethnic conflict in Rwanda – and even in neighbouring Burundi: exclusion of the Hutu majority from power – or from any meaningful participation in the government – by the politically dominant Tutsi minority; and the fear as well as the very real danger of extermination of the Tutsi if they lose power to the Hutu.

The concerns and aspirations of both groups must be addressed if this cycle of violence is to be brought to an end. The alternative is perpetual conflict, hostility or uncertainty, hardly an attractive proposition even if the people of the two embattled nations had never known peace. Given the logic of numbers, it is only a matter of time before the Hutu majority ultimately prevail, with dire consequences for the Tutsi minority, unless the conflict is resolved amicably before it is too late.

A bold initiative is needed even if it entails dissolution of the highly centralised states of Rwanda and Burundi to create a confederation of autonomous ethno-entities or establish independent states of Hutuland and Tutsiland. It is a formidable task, given the nature of the two societies in which the two groups are so integrated and inextricably linked in so many ways including intermarriage through the centuries that they have, virtually, become one people. But it is better than the alternative: war that has no end.

Part Two:

In Retrospect

THE PERPETUAL conflict between the Hutu and the Tutsi in both Rwanda and Burundi raises some fundamental questions as to whether or not something could have been done before or soon after independence to avoid this tragedy.

Should the Belgian colonial rulers, a few years before independence perhaps in the mid-1950s, have restructured or even have redrawn the internal boundaries of the two countries to accommodate conflicting interests and loyalties of the two ethnic groups?

Should the governments of the newly independent nations have done that themselves soon after independence before it was too late? Or should the new leaders have held plebiscites or referendums to ask the Hutu and the Tutsi if they wanted to live together or not, under the same government, or separately and establish their own independent states?

Short of total separation, would extensive devolution of power to the regions or creation of several autonomous entities soon after independence have defused tensions between the two groups and have averted the catastrophe that befell both countries during the early sixties and thereafter?

Similar questions were raised during the Nigerian civil war (1967 – 1970) which almost split the country along ethno-regional lines into independent states because of the domination of the federation by the three main ethnic groups, the Hausa-Fulani, the Igbo and the Yoruba, but especially the Hausa-Fulani who dominated the federal legislature and the army.

The federation also almost broke up because of the seemingly irreconcilable differences between them, mainly between the predominantly Muslim North dominated by the Hausa-Fulani, numerically and politically, and the predominantly Christian South dominated by the Igbo in the Eastern Region and the Yoruba in the Western Region. As Colonel Odumegwu Ojukwu, who led the secession of Eastern Nigeria as the independent Republic of Biafra, stated in August 1968 at the conference of the Organisation of African Unity (OAU) in Addis Ababa, Ethiopia, convened to resolve the conflict:

"The former Federation...encompassed peoples of such vast political, economic, religious and cultural differences as could hardly ever have co-existed peacefully as one independent political entity....

In Northern Nigeria we were physically and socially segregated from the indigenous people. In contrast, the people of Western Nigeria, who shared the same educational and cultural experience, took pride in being 'traditionally reluctant' to settle in and contribute to the development of places outside their Region."[1]

The same could not be said about Rwanda and Burundi. In spite of the hierarchical nature of the Rwandan and Burundian societies dominated by the Tutsi, the Hutu and the Tutsi have never been physically and socially separated from each other as the Igbos and other Easterners, as well as some Westerners, were from the Hausa-Fulani and other people in Northern Nigeria; although even there, there was significant social intermingling – in fact, dynamic cultural and social intercourse in a significant number of ways including intermarriage – between the indigenous Northerners and the "settlers" from the South; a fact conceded by Ojukwu himself:

"We (Igbos and other Easterners but especially Igbos) strove in every way to identify ourselves with the peoples of the areas in which we settled. We spoke their language; we intermarried with them; and Northern Nigerians even declared that, because we wore their dresses, they had conquered us culturally. Yet, in spite of all this, in Northern Nigeria we were physically and socially segregated from the indigenous people."[2]

One significant difference between the two cases – Nigeria and Rwanda/Burundi – is that the Hutu and the Tutsi have, through the centuries, created an integrated society in which the new comers, the Tutsi, long ago adopted the language and the culture of the Hutu majority whom they had conquered and among whom they settled, thus losing their Tutsi identity as a racial, cultural and linguistic community. And in most cases, they even lost their physical features because of intermarriage with the Hutu majority for more than 400 years since they arrived from the north, probably from the Horn of Africa.

That is something the Igbo and other Eastern Nigerians who settled in Northern Nigeria would not have been able to do, even if they wanted to – shed their identity and lose their language and culture the way the Tutsi did – in such a relatively short period (of only a few decades) they had lived in the North contrasted with the centuries during which the Hutu and the Tutsi have lived together in both Rwanda and Burundi.

But there were also some striking parallels between Nigeria and Ruanda-Urundi, as Rwanda and Burundi were known during colonial rule when they were a single territorial entity under the Belgians. There was structural imbalance of both colonial entities – the Nigerian Federation was dominated by the Hausa-Fulani, Ruanda-Urundi by the Tutsi – which led to civil war after the colonial rulers left (in the case of Ruanda even before then).

There was also deep mistrust between the ethnic groups involved, especially on one fundamental question: To whom should power be transferred after the end of colonial rule – to the Hutu or the Tutsi in the case of Ruanda and Urundi? And in the case of Nigeria, to the Hausa-Fulani, the Igbo or the Yoruba, the three dominant groups in the federation whom Achebe calls the tripod on which the nation rests? Power sharing among the dominant groups had proven to be elusive in both cases – Nigeria and Ruanda/Urundi.

In the case of Nigeria, attempts were made by the leaders from all parts of the country (North, East and West) to create more states to replace the three massive regions in order to accommodate the interests of Nigeria's 250 or so ethnic groups on an equitable basis. Had that been done long before independence, in the late 1940s and in the 1950s as advocated by Nnamdi Azikiwe and Chief Obafemi Awolowo, Nigeria would probably have avoided the horrendous tragedy that befell the nation as a result of what was up to then (1967 – 1970) the bloodiest conflict in the history of post-colonial Africa.

Britain, the colonial power, was opposed to such changes or any restructuring of the federation in the forties and fifties. And when independence approached, scheduled for 1960, Nigerian leaders were more interested in assuming power than in restructuring the country to create a stable federation. As chief Anthony Enahoro who was the leader of the Nigerian delegation to the OAU peace talks on the Nigerian civil war stated at the conference in Addis Ababa, Ethiopia, in August 1968:

"During the years of British occupation, Nigeria did not produce one nationalist movement in the classic sense, as was the case in India and Ghana, to mention only two former British colonial territories. Instead, Nigeria produced three nationalist movements which, unfortunately, were based on the three major tribal groupings. The major political parties grew out of these movements, and political developments during the struggle for independence therefore took the shape of compromises between these political parties which were different in their outlook and programmes and which were regionally entrenched. The only common factor among them was the struggle for independence. In their common desire to win independence, many vital problems were left unsolved.

One of these outstanding problems was the creation of more states which would have provided a more lasting foundation for stability of the federation of Nigeria. The British Government pointed out at the time that if new states were to be created, the new states must be given at least two years to settle down before independence could be granted. On reflection, Nigerian leaders have admitted that the British were right and they were wrong on this vital issue in hurrying to independence without solving the problem of stability of the Federation."[3]

In the case of Rwanda and Burundi also, nothing was done to provide a lasting foundation for their stability which should have depended on peaceful co-existence and compromises between the two dominant ethnic groups, the Hutu and the Tutsi. And after independence, nothing was done to guarantee the interests and rights of the powerless in both countries.

In the case of Rwanda, it was the Tutsi who lost power to the Hutu. In Burundi, the Hutu majority remained powerless after the Tutsi took over from the Belgians at independence and went on consolidate their political base and perpetuate themselves in power.

All that was the result of what happened in both countries immediately before independence when each group tried to outmanoeuvre the other and put itself in the best position to seize power from the departing colonial rulers. It depended on who was in the best position to spring first into action.

Also some of the the internal dynamics of the political situation which fuelled problems between the Hutu and the Tutsi were not controlled by these indigenous people. It was the Belgians who were in control. The colonial rulers, as well as the Belgian missionaries, played a very negative role in both Rwanda and Burundi by reinforcing "racial" stereotypes against the Hutu and legitimising Tutsi supremacy over the Hutu majority. The Tutsi, who were the traditional rulers, felt they were better than the Hutu in every conceivable way. The Belgians agreed.

But it was the colonial rulers themselves, as well as the missionaries, who also helped to undermine Tutsi supremacy by providing more opportunities to the Hutu, than they did before, as the two countries approached independence. This helped to embolden the Hutu majority to openly challenge the Tutsi and even rise up against them as happened in Rwanda in 1959.

As independence approached, Rwanda's hereditary ruler Mwami Mutara Rudahigwa III died unexpectedly under suspicious circumstances on 25 July 1959. He was succeeded by his half-brother, Jean-Baptiste Ndahindurwa, who became Mwami Kigeri V.

The Hutu contended that Kigeri had not been properly selected and was incapable of discharging his duties as the new king. Even worse was the fact that many Hutus felt that Mwami Kigeri would be easily manipulated by Tutsi chiefs. They also felt that the chiefs had become more oppressive in recent years, a perception reinforced by rising expectations among the Hutu majority, especially the elite, as a result of the new opportunities that had, relatively speaking, been given to them in the 1950s in anticipation of transfer of power to them as the legitimate democratic majority.

Tragically, the controversy over the royal succession erupted into violence which escalated into civil war between the Hutu and the Tutsi. The Tutsi were supported by the Twa, the smallest ethnic group in the country, who resented the Hutu for having conquered them centuries before the Tutsi came.

The mass uprising by Hutu peasants against their aristocratic rulers, the Tutsi, was a culmination of events preceding Mwami Kigeri's accession to the throne. They had become increasingly dissatisfied with the situation in the country because of their subordinate status as subjects of the Tutsi, a resentment that became a catalyst fuelling the November 1959 uprising.

In only a matter of days, they killed Tutsi chiefs and their auxiliaries – sub-chiefs, headmen, councillors – and virtually destroyed the aristocracy that had been in place for centuries. Tutsi domination finally came to an end and a new era of Hutu supremacy had begun.

Faced with a *fait accompli*, the Belgian colonial rulers appointed Hutu leaders to positions of authority to replace their former masters.

By January 1961, the Hutu were firmly in control of the provisional government, a victory that effectively marked the end of the Tutsi monarchy.

Although the Hutu were now firmly entrenched in power, before and after independence in July 1962, attacks against the Tutsi continued throughout the early 1960s. The ethnic pogroms which began in 1959 claimed tens of thousands of Tutsi lives. Hundreds of thousands more Tutsis ended up as refugees as a result of a tragedy which could have been avoided had the two ethnic groups, with the Belgians acting as mediators, agreed to share power on the basis of a mutually acceptable formula that would have guaranteed the democratic rights of the Hutu majority and security for the Tutsi minority in a genuinely pluralistic context in which they would have enjoyed democratic rights as well in spite of their minority status.

It was one of the darkest periods in Rwandan history. British philosopher and pacifist, Bertrand Russell, called the pogroms which took place just before and after Rwanda's independence "the most horrible and systematic massacre we have had occasion to witness since the extermination of the Jews by the Nazis."[4]

Only a few years later, the massacre of the Tutsi in Rwanda by the Hutu were surpassed by the massacre of the Hutu by the Tutsi in neighbouring Burundi.

The number of Tutsi refugees from Rwanda who fled to neighbouring countries was staggering. It contrasted sharply with the initial euphoria of independence that swept across the continent during the sixties, a period that came to be known as Africa's decade. By the mid-sixties, Uganda alone had about 400,000 refugees from Rwanda, mostly Tutsi. By the early 1990s, their ranks had swelled up to about one million.

It was from this wave of refugees and their offspring that the Rwandan Patriotic Front (RPF) emerged as a potent force that went on to change the course of history not only in Rwanda but in the entire Great lakes region of East Africa. The RPF was led by the Tutsi. It was also dominated by Tutsis. And the vast majority of the fighters in the Rwandan Patroitic Army (RPA), the military wing of the RPF, were Tutsi.

One fundamental question that has to be addressed is

why the events in Rwanda, before and after independence, occurred the way they did.

At the very heart of the conflict was inequity of power between the Hutu and the Tutsi, a subject the Hutu elite passionately addressed in the *Manifesto of the Bahutu* issued in March 1957 and signed by nine Hutu intellectuals. The manifesto was subtitled, *A Note on the Social Aspects of the Indigenous Racial Problem in Rwanda*, and went on to state that the fundamental social and ethnic problem in Rwanda "lies in the political monopoly of one race, the Tutsi race, which, given the present structural framework, becomes a social and economic monopoly....From this to a state of 'cold' civil war and xenophobia, there is only one step."[5]

Thus, the manifesto clearly warned about the potential for a bloody conflict between the Hutu and the Tutsi, although it did not explicitly advocate violence as a solution to the problem. But by making an oblique reference to it, an allusion that was undoubtedly deliberate, the authors of the manifesto did not entirely rule out violence as a viable option in pursuit of their goals.

The tone and content of the manifesto was clearly within the democratic tradition. The implied use of violence contained in the manifesto did not in any way discredit or undermine the document as a declaration of the rights of the Hutu majority to be pursued by democratic means in a pluralistic context.

To prevent violence, the manifesto called for more attention to the inequalities between the Hutu and the Tutsi. It did not emphasise ethnicity as a paramount factor in the disparity but defined the problem in terms of political, economic and social differences between the two ethnic groups.

It demanded specific solutions to poverty, oppression and exploitation of the Hutu majority by the Tutsi minority and urged cooperation of the two groups within the context of an integrated Rwanda transcending ethnicity. And it appealed to the politically dominant Tutsi elite to see to "the integral and collective promotion of the Hutu," and to Belgian colonial rulers to take "more positive and unambiguous measures to achieve the political and economic emancipation of the Hutu."

All those were laudable goals. Few democrats would quarrel with that. Therefore the Hutu manifesto was not revolutionary – let alone violent in rhetoric – reminiscent of the *Communist Manifesto*. It was far from that.

But despite its conciliatory tone, it turned out to be the most revolutionary document ever presented by the Hutu to the Tutsi and the Belgian colonial rulers. For, by demanding equality for the Hutu across the spectrum, although admittedly in a democratic context, and by calling for fundamental change in the country's power structure, economic and social fields, the manifesto tried to destroy the underpinnings of the Tutsi power base.

It was therefore intended to undermine the entire edifice of the Tutsi aristocracy, if all of its demands were to be fulfilled, but without explicitly stating so. In fact, the authors of the manifesto clearly stated that they offered their criticisms and solutions to Rwanda's problems "not at all as revolutionaries" but merely as Rwandans bound together with their fellow countrymen – the Tutsi as well as the Twa and others – in pursuit of a common destiny. Yet the outcome would have been nothing but revolutionary since the manifesto clearly called for a complete overhaul of the system, only in mild language. Also, the ethno-nationalist aspirations of the Hutu majority were clearly embodied in the manifesto.

It was not long after the manifesto was issued that Hutu leaders backed their rhetoric with actions. In June 1957, Grégoire Kayibanda, one of the signers of the manifesto, founded the *Mouvement Social Muhutu* (MSM), a political party dedicated to the fulfillment of the aspirations of the Hutu articulated in the Hutu manifesto.

Kayibanda was one of the members of the Hutu elite who had written articles published in Catholic newspapers in Rwanda about the imperative need for them and other Hutus, the masses in the rural areas, to work together on the basis of ethnic solidarity to achieve common goals. And he went on to become the most prominent figure in the struggle by the Hutu for equality and justice. He also became Rwanda's first prime minister and finally president.

But like all political organisations, the Hutu movement was not entirely united despite its common goals of emancipation and equality. One of the main reasons for such lack of unity was poor communication and organisational links between the elite and the masses in the rural areas. Another major reason was competition among Hutu leaders who offered conflicting visions of a new Rwanda in the post-colonial dispensation in which the Tutsi would no longer be politically dominant.

The leaders included Joseph Gitera who founded the *Association pour la Promotion Sociale de la Masse* (APROSOMA) in October 1957, and Aloys Munyangaju who later became president of the party. APROSOMA was more radically- and populist-oriented than MSM and was even described as "vindictive and messianic" by some observers such as Catherine Newbury in her book, *The Cohesion of Oppression: Clientship and Ethnicity in Rwanda, 1860 – 1890.*[6]

Kayibanda's MSM was more anti-Tutsi in its goals and even rhetoric. But it was Gitera's party, APROSOMA, which worried the Tutsi aristocracy mainly because of its attack on their class status and privileges rather than on their ethnic and cultural identity, the kind of attack that threatened to undermine their hegemonic control over Rwanda. Their class status was virtually synonymous with power.

All these political developments had tragic consequences for Rwanda. They triggered a defensive

137

response from the Tutsi and led to a breakdown of relations between the two ethnic groups as each manoeuvred itself into position to seize power just before or after independence.

In the midst of all this arises a question: Would relations between the two groups have soured so much, to the extent that they did, had the Tutsi conceded the legitimacy of Hutu demands for equality and justice in the late fifties just before independence? Probably not.

But satisfaction of Hutu demands would have entailed radical transformation or the creation of an entirely new Rwanda in terms of power, tipping scales in favour of the Hutu, a disequilibrium that would have relegated the Tutsi to a subordinate position, a status that was alien to them.

The Tutsi would have to surrender power to the Hutu and give up their privileges; an unlikely prospect. And we can only speculate on what would have happened to the Tutsi in the long run even if they had relinquished power to the Hutu voluntarily in 1959 just before the mass uprising of the Hutu peasants that overthrew the Tutsi aristocracy.

But things would probably have been much better especially if – with the participation of the Belgian colonial rulers who were about to depart – a negotiated settlement had been reached to guarantee the rights and security of the Tutsi minority by enabling them to share power with the Hutu in some areas on equal basis and in others on the basis of proportional representation under a Hutu majority government. Unfortunately, nothing even remotely close to that was tried in a substantive manner or was even suggested and, as expected, the Tutsi aristocracy took an uncompromising stand in their response to the Hutus' aggressive demands for equality, a position they forcefully articulated in the following statement issued during those turbulent times:

"The relations between we (Batutsi) and they (Bahutu)

have always until the present been based on servitude. There is, therefore, between we and they no foundation for brotherhood....Since it was our kings who conquered the Bahutu country and killed their petty little kings and thus subjugated the Bahutu, how can they now pretend to be our brothers?"[7]

It was a very insulting and highly inflammatory statement during that volatile period in Rwandan history. And it inflamed passions among the Hutu elite and even among ordinary Hutus who heard the message.

The statement may not have reflected the collective sentiment of the Tutsi leadership and elite; although a tiny minority, there were some liberal and progressive elements among the Tutsi who did not share those views, let alone the incendiary rhetoric fuelled by ethnic bigotry. But the statement captured the essence of what was articulated by the most vociferous and most influential segment of the Tutsi community. That is what the Hutu leaders paid attention to. And that is what they reacted to.

The inflammatory statement by the Tutsi aristocracy was enough to radicalise even some of the most timid and moderate elements among the Hutu since it was clear that they did not intend to share power with the Hutu majority under *any* circumstances.

The conservative leaders among the Tutsi made the situation even worse when they articulated their position in an ethnic context as their statement clearly shows. The imagery they invoked – a glorious past, their "divine" right to rule the Hutu, a perception the Hutu did not share – in that highly provocative statement to justify Tutsi supremacy was racist and gave the Hutu justification to mobilise forces on an ethnic basis instead of pursuing their campaign for justice simply as a political struggle transcending ethnicity.

Such ethnic solidarity among the Hutu was a legitimate response to the exigencies of the situation and was easily defended on pragmatic grounds: as long as we are oppressed as Hutus, the reasoning went, we must mobilise forces as Hutus to fight this oppression. The logic was compelling; so was the sentiment.

Insults only added to injury. According to Tutsi logic, especially the Tutsi aristocracy, the Hutu were conquered because they were inferior, so went the argument. They were given menial jobs because they were less intelligent than the Tutsi. They were kept out of government because they were not capable of governing or leading the country. And they were, of course, ugly because of their dark skin, thick lips, short necks, wide and flat or squashed noses, small and stocky stature.

And because they were, on average, shorter than the Tutsi, they were also short on the grey matter. The list went on and on.

Particularly offensive was the Karinga drum that was kept by the *mwami* – Tutsi king – and literally hanging with the severed genitals of conquered Hutu rulers to symbolise the might and supremacy of Tutsi kings and their "divine" right to rule the subjugated "inferior" Hutus.

Therefore the Hutu movement which might have settled in 1957 for gradual political reform became radicalised by a combination of all those factors and, by 1959, aimed at nothing less than a complete overhaul of the system in a violent revolution aimed at overthrowing the Tutsi aristocracy.

What the Tutsi feared most, loss of power to their subjects and servants the Hutu, thus became a self-fulfilling prophecy mainly because of the Tutsi themselves. They helped to undermine their own regime because of their miscalculations and arrogance and contributed to their dreadful downfall probably as much as the Hutu did. It was a strange alliance of strange bedfellows.

The train of events gained momentum when Mwami Mutara III died in July 1959. When prominent conservative Tutsi leaders immediately chose Jean-Baptiste Ndahindurwa as the new king, they only made things worse.

The Belgian colonial rulers did not agree with the way the succession was handled but, presented with a *fait accompli*, had no choice but to ratify it. But at age 21, and handicapped by other shortcomings including inability to rule, Kigeri V was not the kind of leader who could hold Rwanda together, a country threatened with chaos as a result of political instability caused by inequalities between the Hutu and the Tutsi and fuelled by tensions – which amounted to implacable hostility – between the two groups. The Tutsi themselves were aware of all this and took measures to keep themselves in power by trying to maintain the status quo.

On 15 August 1959, a political party ostensibly of "national unity," was formed by the Tutsi. It was called the *Union Nationale Rwandaise* (UNAR). But there was nothing "national" about it in terms of serving as a vehicle for national unity across ethnic lines. It was basically a Tutsi party intended to preserve, protect and promote Tutsi interests at the expense of the Hutu majority. It had some Hutu members. But it was predominantly Tutsi. And it was pro-monarchy in order to maintain the Tutsi aristocracy in power. It was also anti-Belgian. And for the sake of "national unity," it dismissed the argument that the Tutsi, the Hutu and the Twa were divided along ethnic lines. The party contended that whatever ethnic tensions existed were a product of manipulative colonial policies enforced by the Belgians.

It was a dramatic reversal by a people who had always maintained that they were ordained to rule the inferior Hutus and Twas. The party was clearly intended to neutralise increasing Hutu ethnonationalism in order to perpetuate Tutsi hegemonic control of the country.

It was a period of increasing political agitation and another Tutsi party, the *Rassemblement Democratique*

141

Rwandais (RADER), was formed around the same time. It was smaller and more moderate but had basically the same agenda as the UNAR's. It called for political reforms including democratisation and for a constitutional monarchy unlike the one that existed during that period and which had virtually unlimited powers constrained only by the superimposed structure of colonial rule.

As expected, the Hutu responded with their own mobilisation of forces to pursue their own goals and, at the very least, keep in check a resurgence of Tutsi ethnonationalism especially when the country was moving rapidly towards independence. On 19 October 1959, Grégoire Kayibanda reorganised his party, the *Mouvement Social Muhutu* (MSM), and transformed it into the *Parti du Mouvement de l'Emancipation Hutu* (PARMEHUTU). It was more militant and aimed at mobilising all Hutus across class lines into a cohesive bloc and a potent force under one strong leadership to fulfill Hutu aspirations in a country still dominated by Tutsis.

Tutsi leaders became worried about this new political development and issued a statement denouncing the party as a divisive force in national life. The statement described PARMEHUTU as a party that was "supported by the (colonial) government and the priests" and urged all Rwandans regardless of their tribal or ethnic identities to unite: "Children of Rwanda! Subjects of Kigeri, rise up! Let us unite our strengths! Do not let the blood of Rwanda be spilled in vain. There are no Tutsi, Hutu, Twa. We are all brothers! We are all descendants of Kinyarwanda!"[8]

The contradiction was obvious. All that rhetoric and "patriotism" came from some of the same people who only recently had said the Hutu and the Tutsi were not brothers, had never been brothers, and will never be brothers, as the Tutsi rulers made it clear in their statement quoted earlier. Now, all of a sudden, as their political fortunes began to dwindle, they started chanting, "We are all brothers!"

No one took them seriously; even they themselves

didn't.

The country was already hurtling towards disaster. The battle lines were already drawn.

The most violent confrontations between the Hutu an the Tutsi began on 1 November 1959 when Tutsis associated with the *Union Nationale Rwandaise* (UNAR) attacked a Hutu sub-chief, Dominique Mbanyumutwa, who was a member of PARMEHUTU. The Hutu retaliated by attacking some prominent Tutsi figures including the virulently ant-PARMEHUTU sub-chief, Nkusi. It was the beginning of an inferno that spread and burned across Rwanda for days.

There seemed to have been a pattern that Hutu activists followed in their campaign but no evidence of an orchestrated or coordinated effort directed against the Tutsi. Hutus usually roamed in small gangs to loot and burn Tutsi homes but without killing Tutsis. But that was before the conflict escalated.

At first, the Belgian colonial rulers refused to intervene and rejected the mwami's request on 6 November 1959 to deploy his troops to restore order. The mwami ordered his troops into combat, anyway, mobilising a considerably large force composed of the royal army and militia groups. It was well-coordinated and had one clear objective: to neutralise the Hutu.

Among the targets were Hutu political leaders. Many of them were arrested, tortured or killed.

Hundreds of people were killed in the ensuing strife. Tens of thousands, mostly Tutsi, fled to Burundi, Uganda, Tanganyika (now Tanzania), and Belgian Congo (now the Democratic Republic of Congo, formerly Congo-Kinshasa) where they sought asylum as refugees. Yet this was only the initial phase of the conflict. It was also an ominous sign of what was yet to come.

As the Hutu peasant uprising continued, more people were killed or fled the country. The death toll climbed into tens of thousands. At least 100,000 people were killed in the spiral of violence. Most of them were Tutsi.

The mass uprising completely changed the political configuration of Rwanda in days, not even weeks. The change was that fast and dramatic.

The target of the revolt was not just the Tutsi aristocracy and the political system they had instituted to dominate and exploit the Hutu long before Europeans came but the entire Tutsi community which also benefited from this asymmetrical relationship. Therefore, although the uprising was a revolt, it definitely had revolutionary implications. It changed the system and, by doing so, became a revolution since it was an upheaval and a movement that fundamentally changed the status quo and precluded any possibility of returning to the status quo ante. That is what revolutions do.

Because of the nature of the conflict – fought along clearly defined ethnic lines, Hutu versus Tutsi and vice versa – and the emergence of the Hutu as the new masters of Rwanda, any hope of transforming the country into a genuinely pluralistic society that would accommodate and protect the interests of the defeated Tutsi minority receded into oblivion.

The fate of the Tutsi, as outcasts in the very country they had until recently dominated for centuries, was sealed when the Belgian colonial rulers – who should have acted as impartial mediators, and the final arbiter in the conflict because of their position as the colonial masters – switched sides and started supporting the victorious Hutus who were now guaranteed to be the new rulers, absolute rulers, of Rwanda after the Belgians left on attainment of independence less than two years later in 1962.

Soon after the November 1959 mass uprising, the Belgian authorities arrested three times as many Tutsis as Hutus for plunging the country into chaos and replaced up to 350 Tutsi chiefs with Hutus, most of whom were members of the staunchly pro-Hutu parties, PARMEHUTU and APROSOMA. By early 1960, Hutu controlled almost half (22 out of 45) of Rwanda's chiefdoms and more than half (297 out of 531) of the sub-chiefdoms; a big shift in power in only a few weeks.

The realignment of political forces at the local and regional levels, giving Hutus control over many chiefdoms and sub-chiefdoms and elevating them to other positions of influence and power in anticipation of independence, was immediately followed by other fundamental changes. The most significant one was the reorganisation of Rwanda by the Belgian colonial government. It abolished the 554 chiefdoms and sub-chiefdoms and consolidated them into 229 communes. Elections for the heads of communes – known as *bourgmestres* – and councillors who would work under them were scheduled for July 1960.

The electoral contest itself assumed special significance besides being a quest for public office and an exercise in democracy. The campaign became a struggle for power between the Hutu and the Tutsi as much as it was a referendum on the monarchy, an institution that was detested and reviled by many Hutus, especially the elite, since it symbolised Tutsi supremacy. Because of the extreme tense relations between the two ethnic groups during that period, mainly as a result of the 1959 Hutu peasant revolt against the Tutsi aristocracy only a few months earlier, there were many incidents of violence during the electoral campaign in which both sides suffered. Tutsis died. Hutus also died in the violence.

But it was the Hutu who had the upper hand. And in order to effectively end Tutsi aristocratic rule and prevent a restoration of the status quo ante, three parties – PARMEHUTU, APROSOMA, and the moderate Tutsi-led RADER party which also had Hutu members – formed a united front to wage the campaign against the royalists who supported the aristocracy and who strongly believed in the institution of the monarchy and the right of the Tutsi to rule.

Eventually the Hutu parties, PARMEHUTU and APROSOMA, won by an overwhelming margin. PARMEHUTU was the most successful. And of the major parties, the conservative pro-aristocratic Tutsi *Union Nationale Rwandaise* (UNAR) did the worst. Its humiliating defeat was a strong indictment against the status quo the Tutsi had maintained for more than 400 years to perpetuate themselves in power.

The landslide victory for PARMEHUTU at the polls led to another cataclysmic change when all elected *bourgmestres* and councillors – most of whom were PARMEHUTU members – met in the town of Gitarama in central Rwanda southwest of the capital Kigali on 28 January 1961 to declare and endorse the birth of a nation, "the sovereign democratic Republic of Rwanda."

They also abolished the monarchy and all its symbols, especially the hated Karinga drum decorated with the genitals of Hutu rulers killed by Tutsis.

The assembled delegates declared themselves the Constituent Assembly of Rwanda and chose Dominique Mbanyumutwa as president, and Grégoire Kayibanda as prime minister.

All those changes were confirmed by the electorate – which was overwhelmingly Hutu – in September 1961 when about 80 per cent of the voters cast their ballots in a referendum to abolish the monarchy and enabled PARMEHUTU to win 35 of the 44 seats in Rwanda's new Legislative Assembly.

The changes amounted to a revolution. And the revolution succeeded because the Belgian colonial rulers supported it. They did nothing to stop the 1959 peasant revolt. Instead, they blocked all efforts by the Tutsi traditional rulers to stop the uprising, for instance, by refusing to call out the army which was under the command of Belgian officers serving the colonial government. They also arrested Tutsi counter-insurgents and and dismissed Tutsi chiefs from their posts and replaced them with Hutu appointees.

The Belgian colonial rulers also simply stood by as the leaders and members of the staunchly pro-Hutu PARMEHUTU and other Hutus made a move to seize power.

Because of this attitude on the part of the Belgians, which amounted to tacit approval of what the Hutus were doing, the Hutu leaders who gathered at Gitarama were fully convinced, and rightly so, that the colonial rulers would welcome the establishment of a Hutu-dominated republican form of government to replace the Tutsi monarchy. In fact, the United Nations observers in Rwanda who were sent there to monitor the elections and the country's gradual transition to independence reported that the Belgian colonial administrators not only knew in advance of Hutu plans to seize power from the Tutsi but actually supported them.

Such encouragement by the Belgians, who should have played an impartial role and should have tried to institute power structures which would have accommodated and safeguarded the interests of both ethnic groups, only served to embolden the champions of Hutu ethnonationalism who were determined to exclude the Tutsi from power and other sectors of life; the Tutsi would be allowed to be only subordinates to the new rulers, the Hutu.

Therefore, more than conspiratorial silence but active involvement on the part of the Belgians helped set Rwanda on the path that ultimately led to tragedy including the holocaust more than 30 years later in which almost one million Tutsis perished.

And there was enough evidence even then showing that the country was headed towards catastrophe. Hundreds of thousands of Tutsis had virtually been expelled from their homeland because of the violence directed against them by their fellow countrymen, forcing them to flee to neighbouring countries. It was an experience they would never forget.

Those who remained behind lived in a chronic state of uncertainty, not knowing what to expect or what was coming next or what the future would be. Neither side was innocent. But ethnic violence against the Tutsi continued with official connivance and sanctioned by the belief that those who were being attacked did not belong there; they should go back where they came from – wherever that was (Ethiopia or Somalia, may be?).

Discrimination against the Tutsi became official policy, clumsily disguised as proportional representation but no less malevolent in intent. In March 1961, the United Nations Commission for Ruanda-Urundi issued a report that was highly critical of the direction Rwanda had taken and warned of further trouble:

"A racial dictatorship of one party has been set up in Rwanda, and the developments of the last eighteen months have consisted in the transition from one type of oppressive regime to another. Extremism is rewarded and there is a danger that the [Tutsi] minority may find itself defenseless in the face of abuses."[9]

The oppressor had become the oppressed. And the oppressed had become the oppressor. Violence against the Tutsi continued even after the Hutu had seized almost all the power structures in Rwanda except the colonial infrastructure which remained intact until all power was formally transferred to the Hutu on attainment of independence on 1 July 1962.

Many of the attacks were well-coordinated, had official backing and were sometimes carried out with the participation of the Hutu-dominated army. Others were spontaneous but had the same intent: to intimidate the Tutsi into total submission or drive them out of the country.

But, although outnumbered and outgunned, the Tutsi

responded in kind whenever they could.

However, the odds were against them in a country where they were no longer in power and whose government was dominated by their enemies. They were also vastly outnumbered by the Hutu almost by 8 to 1.

By 1963, the Tutsi who had fled Rwanda and sought refuge in neighbouring countries constituted at least 40% of Rwanda's entire Tutsi population. Some estimates show 70% of the Tutsi fled the country.[10]

This refugee population, seething with anger, constituted a critical mass that was to have a profound impact on Hutu-dominated Rwanda in subsequent years, especially in the early 1990s.

The Tutsi refugees also played a significant role in some of the political developments in the countries where they had settled. Burundi was a prime example.

Militant Tutsi refugees actively participated in Burundi's domestic politics because the country was dominated by fellow Tutsis who allowed their kinsmen from Rwanda to become active participants in the affairs of the country. They played such a major role that they helped determine the course of events in Burundi especially in the area of ethnic relations. They were also involved in making political decisions on the domestic scene and helped shape Burundi's relations with their home country. They were even allowed to use Burundi as a launching pad for their military incursions into Rwanda in an attempt to overthrow the Hutu-dominated regime.

Just as the Tutsi in their halcyon days used ethnicity to bind them together and keep themselves in power, invoking a glorious mythical past and their divine right to rule members of the lesser breed (the Hutu, and by implication, other Bantus) according to their cosmological conceptions, the Hutu employed precisely the same weapon – and their superiority in numbers – to seize power as the rightful owners of the land which had been stolen from them by these invaders "from Ethiopia" who had no more right to be there than the Belgians did.

The tragedy of all this is that nothing was done by the Hutu and the Tutsi themselves, collectively as Rwandans, to debunk these myths and avert future catastrophes. And nothing was done by the Belgian colonial rulers to restructure Rwanda in order to accommodate conflicting interests of the Hutu majority and the Tutsi minority in a genuinely pluralistic context when they were still in power. Instead, the two groups, with the help of their benevolent colonial masters, set out on a collision course that may eventually lead to the destruction of Rwanda as a nation; unless the Hutu are fully included in the government and accorded their democratic rights as the country's majority and the Tutsi are guaranteed full security and citizenship rights in spite of their minority status.

Tragically, no one has devised a mutually acceptable formula that can reconcile the two diametrically opposed sides. To the Hutu, democracy means majority rule, automatically guaranteeing them perpetual control at the expense of the Tutsi. To the Tutsi, such control by the Hutu is synonymous with extermination in a country where they will be powerless and at the mercy of their enemies forever.

Therefore even without mass obliteration, perpetual control by the Hutu is unacceptable to the Tutsi because it would mean subjugation of the minority group; so is perpetual control by the Tutsi equally unacceptable to the Hutu.

Yet, that is the only way the Tutsi believe they can be guaranteed security: control of the country, hence subrdination of the Hutu. Unfortunately, it is a false sense of security in a country where they are vastly outnumbered by the very people whom they want to dominate perpetually in order to be safe, prompting some people including African leaders such as President Daniel arap Moi to suggest that separation of the two is the only solution to this intractable problem.

It is a fate Rwanda shares with its twin, Burundi, although the two differ in some respects.

One of the two areas in which the twin states don't have striking parallels is the way in which they won independence. While the Hutu seized power in Rwanda, the Tutsi remained in control in Burundi before and after independence.

There are other historical differences between the two. The Tutsi in Burundi were not as united as their counterparts were in Rwanda before independence. They were split into the Hima and the Banyaruguru factions, as they still are. Also, unlike Rwanda, Burundi had two dynastic lines: the Bezi and the Batare.

Rwanda was a centralised state under the *mwami*, while Burundi was decentralised to a large degree because of the power wielded by hereditary princes, the *ganwa*. The Belgian colonial rulers in Burundi weakened the *mwami* by strengthening the *ganwa*.

The institution of the monarchy in Burundi survived independence from Belgium. It collapsed in Rwanda about two-and-half years before independence.

And for a few years after independence, Burundi's aristocratic ruler Mwami Mwambutsa IV played a mediating role between the country's contending political forces, Hutu versus Tutsi, and intervened in intra-Tutsi fights which, like the Hutu-Tutsi conflicts, were essentially a struggle for power and often deadly. He had some successes, although probably more failures,[11] but identity politics based on ethnicity remained a primary force that determined the course of events in Burundi.

In Burundi, the decade before independence saw increasing mobilisation of the masses for participation in the political process in anticipation of the departure of the Belgians that would create a political vacuum which would have to be filled by one or both of the indigenous groups, the Hutu or the Tutsi, with the Twa playing

151

virtually no role in the country's political affairs.

In 1957, the Tutsi formed a political party known as *Parti de l'Unite et du Progres National* (UPRONA). It was led by Chief Leopold Bihumugani who was also known as Biha. The leaders of UPRONA were members of the Bezi dynastic line and allies of the *mwami*, hence beneficiaries of the existing political system.

The primary reason for forming the party was to oppose the colonial policies and other proposed changes which would have reduced the power of the *mwami* – also, by extension, of the Bezi chiefs allied with him – and benefited their opponents belonging to the Batare dynastic line. Compounding the problem, of intra-Tutsi rivalry, was the fact that Batare leaders supported these changes, and for good reason. They were not allies of the *mwami*, Mwambutsa IV.

UPRONA was not only staunchly pro-monarchy; its leader after 1958 was Prince Louis Rwagasore, the eldest son of Mwami Mwambutsa IV, who was also a *ganwa* (princely) representative of the Bezi. Yet UPRONA was not an ethnic party, *per se*, forcefully articulating and defending Tutsi hegemonic interests. It was, instead, a party of "national unity" although it was led by and served the interests of an aristocratic elite from the Bezi dynasty. But it tried to shed its Tutsiness by appealing to all Burundians regardless of their ethnic identity and even had some Hutu leaders. In fact, Prince Rwagasore himself was known for being sympathetic towards the Hutu and even had Hutu physical features although he was a Tutsi.

Not to be outdone by their opponents, members of the Batare branch also formed their own party, *Parti Démocrate Chrétien* (PDC), under the leadership of Joseph Biroli and Joseph Ntitendereza. Biroli, like Rwagasore, had been educated in Europe and was one of the enlightened chiefs not strictly bound by tradition in his political outlook.

The PDC was more progressive, contrasted with the

aristocratic-oriented UPRONA, and addressed a number of social issues affecting the general wellbeing of Burundians across the spectrum. It also attracted more educated Burundians but was less inclined to demand immediate independence. Those were qualities and attributes which pleased the Belgian colonial authorities who became more friendly towards PDC than UPRONA.

During the communal elections of November 1960, the Belgians placed Prince Rwagasore under house arrest, enabling PDC to dominate the electoral contest. It won 942 of the 2876 contested seats. UPRONA won 545.

It was dirty politics but expedient for the colonial rulers.

It was around the same time that neighbouring Rwanda was going through a convulsion following the Hutu peasant revolt, or mass uprising, that had taken place the year before and which had a direct impact on Burundi's domestic scene in terms of ethnic relations. The cataclysmic event reverberated through the years and throughout the region, with ethnic violence in Rwanda especially through the sixties sending waves of Tutsi refugees into Burundi. Forcibly exiled from their homeland, they were filled with animosity towards the Hutu and plotted to turn back the tide and oust their enemies from power as soon as possible.

The mass exodus of Tutsis from Rwanda alarmed their tribal kinsmen in Burundi who feared for their own survival should the Hutu seize power as they had done next-door. They "reasoned that if this was the way that the Hutu behaved once they had obtained power, then this is what would happen in Burundi if the Hutu were to become dominant."[12]

The other factor impinging on Burundi's domestic political scene was itself domestic. Mwami Mwambutsa IV and members of the Bezi dynastic line feared that should a revolution take place in Burundi and lead to the formation of a republican form of government, that would be the end of the monarchy. Therefore supporters of the monarchy such as UPRONA did everything they could to maintain aristocratic rule by welcoming reforms that would at least guarantee a constitutional monarchy instead of abolishing it.

They also appealed across ethnic lines to bring the Hutu and the Tutsi together in a spirit of national unity in order to maintain the integrity of Burundi as a political entity that guaranteed equality for all under a constitutional monarchy. And Mwami Mwambutsa himself started playing an activist role in national politics. He claimed to be non-partisan but, as he became more directly involved in politics, he used his position to exert significant influence on the course of events to his advantage. By doing so, he compromised his status as an impartial figure who was above partisan politics and who loomed large on the political scene that had always been dominated by chiefs and *ganwa* princes who had no dominant figure among them.

The king's direct involvement in politics alienated many people: members of the Batare dynasty who were already against him; his allies in the Bezi dynasty; ordinary Tutsis and, of course, Hutus who had always been dominated by their conquerors. But because he tried to reach out to all groups in the country, he agreed to fulfill some political demands by the Hutu, a concession that alienated many of his fellow Tutsis.

He tried to juggle conflicting interests in order for Burundi to attain sovereign status without going through a violent upheaval and without replacing the monarchy with a republican system which derives its mandate from the electorate. He succeeded in doing so but with unintended consequences. Although the monarchy survived, the leaders of the country's two main political parties did not.

In September 1961, Burundi held parliamentary elections in anticipation of independence the following year. UPRONA trumpeted its themes of national unity and constitutional monarchy to mobilise forces across ethnic lines in a spirit of national solidarity that enabled it to win an overwhelming victory at the polls. It won 80% of the vote and 58 out of 64 seats in the Legislative Assembly. The Hutu, who constitute the majority of the population, played a major role in its victory although years later, the party became pro-Tutsi and virulently anti-Hutu.

UPRONA celebrated its victory. But it turned out to be a sour victory. Not long after the elections, the leader of UPRONA, Prince Louis Rwagasore who had always been sympathetic towards the oppressed Hutu majority, was assassinated on 31 October 1961 in a plot that eventually led to the execution of PDC's leaders, Joseph Biroli and Joseph Ntitendereza as well as three others. Thus in a single swoop, both of the major parties were decapitated, creating a vacuum of leadership that became very difficult to fill.

However, the monarchy remained intact. So, Burundi emerged from colonial rule on 1 July 1962 (the same day Rwanda also won independence) having been spared the agony of a violent mass uprising that ushered in a new era of republican rule in Rwanda after centuries of aristocratic rule.

Although Burundi won independence with its monarchy intact, that was still after a republican model had been put in place in Rwanda following the 1959 peasant revolt, thus drawing a lot of interest from Burundi's Hutus who wanted to emulate their kith-and-kin next-door. This led to increased tensions between the Hutu and the Tutsi in Burundi.

And while the struggle for power among the Tutsi themselves had always drawn a lot of attention, the death of three main Tutsi leaders – Rwagasore, Biroli and Ntitendereza – shifted the focus, even if temporarily, to the competition between the Hutu and Tutsi although intra-Tutsi rivalry remained a factor in Burundian politics. And Mwami Mwambutsa IV continued to intervene in politics, ostensibly as a mediator. For example, from the early to mid-sixties, he appointed Hutu and Tutsi prime ministers to satisfy both groups.

But his intervention was seen by elected officials – Hutu and Tutsi – as unwarranted interference in the democratic process, and the threat of a Hutu revolution patterned after the republican model next-door in Rwanda was a constant worry among many Tutsis.

However, this fear among the Tutsi in Burundi that the Hutu would seize power and destroy the monarchy as happened in Rwanda was sometimes overshadowed by intrigues in domestic politics between the Tutsi rulers themselves.

Even the hope of a peaceful transition from colonial rule to sovereign status was dashed as relations between the Hutu and the Tutsi became increasingly violent.

The volatile situation got worse because of independence itself. That was because independence led to rising expectations and intense competition for jobs and other benefits, a rivalry – between the Hutu and the Tutsi – in which the *mwami* regularly intervened as mediator. And unlike Rwanda, Burundi was firmly under Tutsi control. In fact, the country won independence under Tutsi leadership whose apex was the *mwami* himself.

But cleavages among the Tutsi themselves sometimes opened up opportunities for Hutus. Such was the case in June 1963 when the prime minister, a Tutsi, resigned. He complained about Mwami Mwambutsa's interference in the conduct of national affairs, making it very difficult for the government to discharge its responsibilities. He was replaced by a Hutu, Pierre Ngendadumwe. But like his Tutsi predecessor, he did not last long in office. It was the mwami's responsibility to appoint and replace prime ministers, a powerful role he used to balance competing interests between the Hutu and the Tutsi and enhance his position.

Between 1963 and 1965, Burundi had five different

156

governments, each with Hutu and Tutsi cabinet members, although not in proportional numbers to reflect the demographic composition of this bifurcated state. It was an unstable political situation. But it enabled Mwami Mwambutsa IV to wield undue influence. His political dexterity and manipulation did, somewhat, balance competing interests of the Hutu and the Tutsi. But it pleased neither side as each tried to manoeuvre itself into the most advantageous position to have the greatest influence in the government and, if possible, take full control of the country.

Therefore, in addition to appeasing no one, the mwami's intervention only suspended, temporarily, the political conflict between the two ethnic groups that everyone saw coming, with dire consequences for the country. The Belgian colonial rulers did nothing to prevent this impending disaster which they also saw coming as the country approached independence. They let the country continue to be dominated by the Tutsi minority at the expense of the Hutu majority, while in Rwanda, they let the Hutu seize power while ignoring the interests and security of the Tutsi minority.

It was a tragic mistake in both cases. Had it been corrected at that time, probably neither country would have degenerated into chaos. And probably neither would have been torn by civil war during the next several decades.

This was one perfect example of the evils of colonialism and reminds one of what Walter Rodney, the author of *How Europe Underdeveloped Africa* which he wrote when he was teaching at the University of Dar es Salaam in Tanzania, said about this system of imperial domination, oppression and exploitation. He stated in his book: "The only positive development in colonialism was when it ended."

Rwanda and Burundi are some of the African countries which have suffered most and which continue to suffer from the devastating impact of imperial conquest, the conflict between the Hutu and the Tutsi being one of the legacies of colonial rule because of the way the Belgians administered those countries, encouraging the Tutsi to oppress the Hutu in both Rwanda and Burundi and then taking sides with the Hutu in Rwanda to oppress the Tutsi as the country approached independence.

In Burundi, the dissatisfied Hutu majority led by the elite began to demand what they felt were their rights as the country's majority. The Hutu leaders who led this campaign were familiar with the policies and tactics of Rwanda's ruling republican party, PARMEHUTU, or had ties to it. Yet such identification with a staunchly pro-Hutu party next-door meant that the ideological underpinnings of the Hutu struggle for equality in Burundi would also assume an ethnic dimension, just like in Rwanda, thus confirming the fear among the Tutsi in Burundi that the same thing that happened to their kinsmen in Rwanda would happen to them if the Hutu became their rulers.

Therefore increasing Hutu militancy in Burundi provoked an opposite and equally strong reaction, Tutsi extremism, in spite of the fact that such political agitation by the Hutu was essentially for democratic rights and equality with the Tutsi. Whatever the case, the context was set for a deadly conflict between the two groups.

The process of strong ethnic identification in Burundi's politics by Hutu leaders was also fuelled by racial and historical arguments similar to what happened in Rwanda and telescoped into this: oppression by Tutsis, a "Nilotic" people or whatever they were (even "Caucasoid"), who came from the north and subjugated the Hutu, a people of Bantu stock, was intolerable and must be stopped.

The logic was compelling and there was nothing fictitious about it. It was a historical fact. The oppression of the Hutu by the Tutsi was also contemporary reality. What was fictitious was the contention by the Tutsi political leaders during the sixties, and just before independence, that there were no "ethnic" differences between the two groups, that they got along just fine, and that tribalism was an alien ideology that was invented by the colonial rulers; conveniently ignoring the fact that there was tribalism in Burundi, and Rwanda, as well as in other parts of Africa long before Europeans came although it is true that they encouraged it and used it keep Africans divided in order to control and dominate them. And although it was true that the differences between the two groups was not biological, they did exist as separate entities, each with its own identity, Hutu or Tutsi, hence as ethnic categories.

The Tutsi political leaders also ignored the fact that probably more than anything else, it was the Tutsi themselves who ruled Burundi – as much as they did Rwanda – for centuries; inequity of power that was justified on "racial" grounds by the Tutsi themselves who contended that they were superior to the subjugated Hutus in every conceivable way. Now, as a matter of expediency, they changed the tune, just before and after independence, to protect themselves because of their precarious position as a very small minority in a country where – if democratic principles were genuinely applied – their subjects, the Hutu, would end up on top as their rulers on the basis of majority rule.

The choices were stark and clear, and frightening, for the Tutsi: concede defeat through the ballot box and let the Hutu majority rule – or continue to dominate the Hutu and risk chaos and war.

Nothing seemed capable of defusing the increasing tension between the two groups. The situation was exacerbated by Mwami Mwambutsa who continued to play his supposedly balancing role as an impartial mediator between the Hutu and the Tutsi.

In 1965, another general election was held that was to have far-reaching consequences for Burundi and the entire Great Lakes region. Hutu candidates won 23 out of 33 seats in a country where, like Rwanda, they constituted an overwhelming majority, at least 85 per cent of the total population as they still do today. Therefore the results reflected a genuine, democratic choice of the majority of the voters.

But the Tutsi king (*mwami*), Mwambutsa IV, refused to accept a Hutu who was chosen by the majority of the members of the national legislature to be the new prime minister; the legislature was predominantly Hutu. Instead, he appointed a Tutsi prince who was close to him to be the prime minister and tried to increase his own influence over the government and in other areas of Burundi's political arena. It was an act of blatant injustice to the Hutu majority and virtual repudiation of the election results, by the monarch, hence by the Tutsi leadership he led and represented.

In response to that, a group of Hutu army officers tried to depose the king on 18 October 1965. But the coup attempt failed and provoked an extremely brutal response from the Tutsi-dominated government and royalist army which was also predominantly Tutsi.

All fears of a bloody ethnic conflict between the two groups were now being realised in an orgy of killings that followed the abortive coup attempt.

At least 34 Hutus who participated in the coup attempt were immediately arrested and executed. But the retaliatory response by the Tutsi went much further than that. Almost all Hutu soldiers and officers were expelled from the army – and many more – were killed at different times thereafter. Also, Hutu politicians and government officials were arrested. Many of them were shot dead.

Ethnic violence flared up across the country in retaliatory campaigns by both sides. And the Tutsi-dominated army launched an extremely brutal campaign as part of a scorched-earth policy by the government to neutralise Hutus, killing them indiscriminately. Thousands perished. A conservative estimate put the casualty figure at

160

5,000.

Two weeks after the failed coup attempt, Mwami Mwambutsa IV left for Europe on 2 November 1965, having given up all efforts trying to accommodate the interests of the two groups who were virtually at war. He never returned to Burundi.

He left no effective government when he left. And his departure, according to royal sources, was said to be an abdication in favour of his son and heir-apparent, Prince Charles Ndizeye, who was reportedly put in charge of the country by his father to manage affairs in the king's absence.

But it was actually a coup engineered by Tutsi army officers led by Captain Michel Micombero who were opposed to the monarchy and who used the mwami's 19-year-old son as a front to seize power.

Even when he acceded to the throne, the juvenile prince – some sources say he was 21 at the time – did not become king. He was a regent but the military ruled for him until they realised they could rule the country without him. He was deposed on 28 November 1965 when he was out of the country.

Prince Charles, then crowned as Mwami Ntare V, became yet another expendable commodity in Burundi's internecine political wars. And his ouster led to the immediate proclamation of Burundi as a republic by the young Tutsi military elite.

Initially, the change seemed to have been justified. The monarchy was abolished, raising prospects for a transition to a new dispensation in which democratic rule would prevail. But the new regime – almost all Tutsi – soon became a brutal dictatorship whose brutality and abuse of power had no parallel in Burundi's history.

The military coup by Tutsi army officers, and the skillful manipulation of different groups and individuals by Mwami Mwambutsa IV which effectively kept power in the hands of the Tutsi, sidelined the Hutu and kept them on the periphery of the mainstream; helped Burundi, although in a tragic way, avoid full-scale confrontation between the Hutu and the Tutsi because the Hutu had been rendered powerless with the expulsion of Hutu army officers and soldiers from the army and with the elimination of many of Hutu leaders; and prevented Tutsi princes, the *ganwa*, from regaining a foothold in the political arena they had always dominated together with the *mwami* as the aristocratic elite.

But even with the absence of the Tutsi princes from the political arena as effective players, the new players – the young military officers who constituted the new regime under a republican system which had replaced the monarchy – were also Tutsi and therefore ensured that Burundi's politics and the entire national life would still be dominated by Tutsis.

Intra-Tutsi rivalry also continued in the post-aristocratic era. The new Tutsi military rulers were mostly from the southwestern region of Bururi, a Hima area, where Micombero and the majority of his fellow army officers were born. Their biggest rivals were fellow Tutsis from another region, Muramvya, in central Burundi. It is these two factions that came to dominate Burundi's politics. The Hutu were virtually shunted into oblivion and trapped in the political crossfire between the two contending forces.

The rival groups, united only by their common Tutsi identity and their desire to keep Hutus on the periphery, had two paramount goals: political supremacy over the other and the rest of the country; and exclusion of the Hutu from power. These objectives were inexorably linked to perpetuation of Tutsi supremacy and led to tragic consequences for the country including a series of genocidal attacks on the Hutu in the next several decades. Neighbouring Rwanda was also wracked by violence during the same period but mainly against the Tutsi.

The conflicts in Rwanda and Burundi had similar yet

different characteristics. They were basically a struggle for power – but with strong ethnic biases.

In Rwanda, the ethnic divide between the Hutu and the Tutsi was more pronounced in terms of power allocation and social status than in Burundi where the Tutsi princes, the *ganwa*, often collectively identified Tutsi commoners and all Hutus as basically the same subjects who belonged to the same class. By remarkable contrast, in Rwanda class consciousness among the Tutsi – from the most humble to the most exalted – all of them as members of the upper or higher caste (above all Hutus) in a highly stratified society precluded that possibility.

And because of the strong and sharp ethnic distinctions in Rwanda, ethnic conflict in that country started earlier and more decisively than it did in Burundi. The battle lines were clearly drawn long before mass violence erupted in 1959 on an unprecedented scale and shook Rwandan society to its very foundation, destroying the institution of the monarchy which was the pillar of that hierarchical society.

The Tutsi who fled Rwanda and sought refuge in Burundi and other neighbouring countries intensified ethnic hostilities when they launched a series of invasions, especially from Burundi, to try to regain power from the Hutu. The first major invasion took place in November 1963. It was launched from Burundi but failed to dislodge the Hutu who were securely anchored in power. A second and better coordinated invasion came a month later. On 21 December 1963, Tutsi fighters – derisively called *Inyenzi* (cockroaches) by the Hutu – began to infiltrate Rwanda from their sanctuaries in Burundi, Uganda, Tanganyika and Congo. They used several entry points. But not all their plans were successful.

However, a significant number of them entered Rwanda, triggering a vicious response from the Hutu-dominated Rwandan army led by Belgian officers. The military counterattack was supported by Hutu peasants and other civilians who retaliated against the Tutsi across the country. About 15,000 Tutsis were killed. Among them were 20 prominent Tutsis whose names were "on a list of prospective future ministers in a Tutsi-led government that had been found on the body of one of the attackers."[13]

The Hutu army and civilian fighters beat back the invaders. But the invasion, like the incursions before, only inflamed passions among the Hutu majority. And the harsh retaliatory response against Tutsis in general also fuelled ethnic animosity between the two groups, paving the way for more violence. There was nothing that could stop the conflict from escalating. Both sides took an uncompromising stand on the fundamental issues that divided them and which continued to divide them 40 years later.

While Rwanda was fighting her own battles in the sixties, Burundi was also embroiled in her own but which diverged from the path taken by the civil strife next-door and had less of an ethnic component than Rwanda's next door.

After Micombero and his colleagues seized power in 1966, they went on to consolidate their position, jealously protecting their privileges, and suppressed any kind of opposition to their rule. Whether Hutu or Tutsi, real or imagined, any opposition triggered a harsh response from the military regime, a clique of army officers from Bururi who were members of the Hima branch of Tutsis found throughout the Great Lakes region and who include Ugandan President Yoweri Museveni. He is a member of the Banyankole ethnic group indigenous to southwestern Uganda which is a branch of the Hima and is a close ally of the Tutsi rulers of Rwanda whom he helped to seize power in July 1994 when they launched their successful invasion from Uganda to oust the genocidal Hutu regime of President Juvénal Habyarimana.

In the late sixties, a bitter intra-Tutsi rivalry erupted between the Bururi and the Muramvya factions which even sometimes overshadowed the animosity between the Hutu and the Tutsi; Muramvya is a central and Waruguru area.

The Bururi ruling clique was known for being anti-aristocratic and anti-Hutu. It saw the monarchy and the Hutu – with their demand for democratic rights and majority rule – as a dual threat to its hegemonic control of the country. And it is true that the Hutu tried several times in the late sixties and early seventies to end Tutsi domination in Burundi.

In 1969, as relations between the Hutu and the Tutsi continued to deteriorate rapidly, Micombero's government arrested large numbers of Hutus to foil a coup attempt. The alleged plot was uncovered in late 1969. In response to that, many Hutu leaders were killed, including Hutu army officers and soldiers. And almost all the rest of the Hutu in the army were expelled.

Having neutralised the Hutu, at least temporarily, the Bururi faction of President Micombero's Tutsis now turned on fellow Tutsis of the Muramvya faction whom Micombero and his colleagues accused of having ties to the monarchy and the Hutu. And there was some truth to the claim that the Muramvya faction had ties to the ousted monarchy.

During Mwami Mwambutsa's reign, a number of Tutsis of the Muramvya group held privileged positions and may have wanted to see the monarchy restored. By 1970, President Micombero and other Tutsis in the government from his home region were convinced that the Muramvya group posed a serious threat to their regime and the republican system and began to crack down on them. The campaign was vicious.

Many Tutsis from Muramvya were arrested, beaten, tortured, and killed. Others were subjected to show trials dispensing kangaroo justice, with some of them being sentenced to death. The victims came from all walks of life. And they had only one thing in common: coming from Muramvya.

The campaign of terror by the government against the Muramvya Tutsis was so bad and systematic that it almost ignited a civil war between the two groups and raised the possibility of a revolt by the Hutu whom many feared would take advantage of the situation to seize power while the Tutsi, the rulers of the land, were busy fighting among themselves.

The return of Mwami Ntare from exile on 30 March 1972 only made things worse. Micombero's government believed that Ntare, a symbol of the monarchy, had the sympathy and support of its bitter enemies, the Tutsi of the Muramvya faction.

It is said that President Micombero himself guaranteed Mwami Ntare safety if he returned to Burundi, but some government advisors recommended that he should be executed immediately. There were analysts who said that the decision to execute Mwami Ntare was intended to prod the Hutu into an uprising and incite the pro-monarchy Muramvya Tutsis also to rise up against the government and provide the regime with an excuse to eliminate its opponents. Whatever the case, that is almost exactly what happened after Micombero dissolved his cabinet on 29 April 1972.

Within hours on April 29th, violence erupted in three different regions of Burundi, a strong indication that the attacks were coordinated. Hutu rebels in southern Burundi, probably with logistical and material support from Congolese insurgents (waging their own war against President Mobutu Sese Seko's brutal and kleptocratic regime), launched an attack in which hundreds of Tutsis were killed. They swept through the southern part of the country, indiscriminately killing Tutsis. It was estimated that the number of Tutsis killed was 500 to 3,000.

The number of casualties was deliberately kept vague by the government as part of a disinformation campaign augmented by inflated official numbers to blame the Hutu for a much larger massacre of Tutsis – which never took place – in order to justify its brutal repression of the Hutu majority whose casualties exceeded 200,000 and may even have reached 300,000 according to some sources.

The large number alone, of 200,000 to 300,000 casualties, clearly points to civilian involvement, Tutsis armed by the Tutsi government to kill Hutus with the help of the Tutsi army. Without civilian involvement, ordinary Tutsis helping the Tutsi army to kill Hutus all over the country, the number of casualties may have been lower. Tutsi civilians were given machetes by the government to kill Hutus, the same way the Hutu government did in Rwanda years later when it distributed machetes among the Hutu to slaughter Tutsis across the country in large numbers within a relatively short period of time. The massacre of Hutus in Burundi was, in terms of style and intent, a precursor to what was to took place in Rwanda about two decades later.

It was genocide in every sense of the word. But it hardly made international headlines.

People talk about genocide by the Hutu against the Tutsi in Rwanda, especially the 1994 holocaust, but they hardly talk about genocide by the Tutsi against the Hutu in both Rwanda and Burundi through the years.

With regard to the conflict in Burundi in 1972, another important factor was the timing of the attack, coincidental or not. Had Micombero not dissolved his cabinet on April 29th, the attack may not have taken place; or it still may have, on a different date, and with less coordination.

April 29th was a Saturday, a traditional market day in Burundi when large numbers of people are out buying things, enabling the rebels to mobilise forces and pile up weapons and move them around without anyone paying attention to their movements and activities. They were just a part of the crowd that was out there on that particular day, mingling, buying and selling, as they had always done traditionally.

The American ambassador to Burundi during that time, Thomas Melady, said about 4,000 to 5,000 Hutus took part in the initial campaign. Their main targets were military installations, police stations, and the government-controlled radio station which is always a prime target in military coups across Africa and elsewhere. As he states in his book, *Burundi: The Tragic Years*:

"Cars were being stopped...and people were being dragged out from their cars and killed....(But the organised campaign degenerated into) a mass chaos of settling scores between individuals....(The official interpretation of these events was) that Burundian (Hutu) armed rebels allied with Zairian exiles (Mulelists, followers of Pierre Mulele, Patrice Lumumba's education minister and heir-apparent) attacked southern Burundi, Gitega, and Bujumbura (the capital) on April 29 – 30; that about 5,000 people were killed and that they were mostly Tutsi...(also that) the goal of the invading force was to establish a Hutu-dominated republic and to liquidate the Tutsi."[14]

Ambassador Melady disputed this official version of events by the Burundian government. He contends that about 1,000 to 2,000 people were killed.

One of the victims was Mwami Ntare. He was executed while under house arrest by a government official named Shibura on the very night that the fighting erupted.

The assassination of Mwami Ntare was a deliberate act by Micombero's government which feared that his presence on Burundi's highly volatile political scene would incite and encourage the Hutu and the Muramvya faction of Tutsis to join forces and help the ousted young king – who served as a rallying point for opposition to the military junta – reinstitute the monarchy, thus ending republican rule introduced by Micombero and his colleagues.

It was the same fear of insecurity that prompted the government to respond to the rebellion with extremely brutal repression. Hutus were indiscriminately slaughtered in many parts of the country regardless of whether or not they supported the revolt or even knew about it. In some areas, the killings were specific. Hutus identified as intellectuals – teachers, students, and others with some education or money – were summarily executed.

Not only did President Micombero's Tutsi government exaggerate the scale of the uprising, as well as the degree of foreign involvement, claiming that more than 50,000 Tutsis were massacred by the Hutu; the regime even knew about the revolt in advance but did nothing to stop it so that the government would have an excuse to kill Hutus in large numbers. In fact, Tutsi teachers and students even helped prepare lists of their Hutu colleagues and schoolmates for elimination by government soldiers and hit squads of Tutsi thugs.

It was a massive, genocidal campaign by the Tutsi government against the Hutu, ostensibly in self-defence, and a retribution against the insurgents:

"The most reliable estimates of casualties hold that at least 80,000, and perhaps as many as 300,000, Hutus were murdered in 1972.

The Tutsi regime that perpetrated these massacres survived for several years afterwards (until 1976) and, therefore, was able to prevent an accurate death count."[15]

There is a tendency among some analysts to describe the killings as mutual genocide, Hutus killing Tutsis and Tutsis killing Hutus. And there are those who blame the Hutu for starting the violence in Burundi in 1972. But they ignore or simply overlook the context in which the violence erupted and what motivated the Hutu – against overwhelming odds, given the fact that they were powerless, while their adversaries controlled the government and the army – to rise up against the regime.

These were the people who had never ruled Burundi or themselves after they were conquered by the Tutsi hundreds of years ago and who, after losing power, became virtual slaves of their conquerors who systematically oppressed and exploited them and even considered them to be inferior. And despite their attempts to change the system by peaceful means through the years, they were only met with brutal repression at the hands of their Tutsi rulers.

Also, the 1972 Hutu rebellion is not looked at in its proper context from a proportional perspective. There was gross disproportion in the scale of the killings and of the forces and firepower involved. Burundi's government, dominated by the Tutsi, and the army, also dominated by the Tutsi, orchestrated and led the genocidal campaign against the Hutu and fully supported and armed Tutsi civilians in their murderous rampage against their fellow citizens who only happened to be members of a different group; the same way the Hutu government, and the Hutu army, did to the Tutsi in Rwanda decades later.

In contrast, the number of Hutu rebels who launched the attack against the Tutsi was comparatively smaller even though the insurgents were joined by some of their civilian kinsmen in the campaign.

But the violence on their part, and the firepower they had, came nowhere close to the ferocity of the campaign by the Tutsi against them who had the support of the army and other security forces including the police, a disproportion that invalidates the government's contention that the regime was only acting in self-defence when it launched its brutal offensive against the Hutu including civilians in pursuit of its scorched-earth policy that earned it the unenviable distinction as one of the bloodiest and most brutal regimes in the history of post-colonial Africa:

"The Hutu murderers, at some level, feared the

consequences of a Hutu uprising, but most of the killings did not occur in an atmosphere of frightened frenzy. According to survivor accounts, some of the killings probably involved individuals settling personal scores. But the overwhelming majority of Hutus were murdered in a planned, cold, and calculating way. The government did not, as Micombero claimed, seek out only the guilty; the government's reprisal was comprehensive and systematic, and probably planned well before the Hutu uprising of April 29, 1972.

Many Hutus were taken from their homes at night; others reported to police stations in response to misleading requests. The government-supported killers frequently used machetes and did not rely heavily on bullets, a foreshadowing of machete massacres by Hutus against Tutsis that would take place twenty-two years later in Rwanda, in 1994.

The 1972 genocide included many Hutu peasants among its victims, but the primary target was the modern class of Hutus – priests, teachers, managers, clerks. The Tutsi ruling class struck against a contending elite. The preferred victims fell into four categories: (1) Hutus with government jobs; (2) Hutu soldiers; (3) Hutus who were wealthy – those with bank accounts, those whose homes had iron roofs; and (4) Hutus with some secondary or college education. The Tutsi government intended to eliminate all Hutu competition for leadership of Burundi for at least the next decade.

For the most part, the Tutsis succeeded in this objective. Although tensions between Hutus and Tutsis did not go away, and the Micombero government fell in 1976 to a coup led by another Tutsi, Lieutenant-Colonel Jean-Baptiste Bagaza, the decimated Hutu population lost its ability to mount a serious threat to Tutsi rule for about fifteen years."[16]

One of the most disturbing aspects of the 1972 genocide against the Hutu in a campaign of state-sponsored terror was the lack of an international response to the tragedy, especially within Africa itself. I remember the massacres well. I was in Dar es Salaam, Tanzania, during that period. The country's main newspaper, the *Daily News*, provided ample coverage of the massacres.

Nothing was done to stop the killings. There was, instead, widespread support across the continent for Burundi's brutal regime. And the Organisation of African Unity (OAU) accepted the government's claim that "the situation in Burundi was primarily the result of outside aggression sponsored by neocolonial forces. The (Burundian) delegation also claimed that tribalism was not a factor in the Burundi crisis and that Burundi had achieved a 'tribal homogeneity unparalleled in Africa.'"[17]

The claim was utter nonsense, coming from leaders whose hands were dripping with blood after waging one of the deadliest campaigns of ethnic cleansing in modern history.

Opposed to military coups and out of African solidarity, Tanzania – although she still welcomed Hutu refugees fleeing from persecution in Burundi as much as she welcomed Tutsis fleeing from Hutu persecution in Rwanda – sent arms and ammunition to help defend Burundi's government. And Zaire deployed paratroopers to reinforce the Tutsi-dominated army and security forces.

But even if African governments had good intentions when they supported Micombero's government, the Hutu in Burundi felt betrayed and forsaken even by fellow Africans at a time when they desperately needed help to save their lives.

Many Tutsis in Burundi even contemplated mass obliteration of the Hutu as a desirable solution. That was more than 20 years before the Hutu tried use the same solution with the Tutsi in neighbouring Rwanda. As Jack David Eller states in his book, *From Culture to Ethnicity to Conflict*:

"Many Burundian Tutsi now saw the Hutu as *the* enemy and the total eradication of Hutu leaders – and maybe of the Hutu people – as the only solution, the 'final solution,' to Burundi's problems."[18]

And in the words of René Lemarchand in his work, *Burundi: Ethnocide as Discourse and Practice*:

"The killing of Hutu seemed to have become part of the civic duty expected of every Tutsi citizen."[19]

The brutal subjugation of the Hutu in Burundi, including confiscation of their property, led to a period of unchallenged Tutsi supremacy for almost an entire generation, although it did not lead to stability let alone national unity.

By 1987, Hutus had begun to make some progress in different areas. But blatant discrimination still kept them in a subordinate position. They were given very limited opportunities in education and employment, and only a few minor positions in the government, and in the army, the country's most powerful institution as is the case in almost all African countries.

A military coup in late 1987 which brought Major Pierre Buyoya to power raised some hope among the Hutu that their condition would improve, even if only slightly, for the first time since 1972. Buyoya seemed to be genuine in his intentions to improve ethnic relations and end the bloodshed. But while the change in government encouraged Hutus' demands for equality, it frightened Tutsis who felt that any improvement of conditions for the Hutu would undermine their position. That has always been the fear among Tutsis, losing power, status and influence to the Hutu.

But Burundi was once again plunged into chaos and

bloodshed only a few months later in 1988 not long after Buyoya seized power from his cousin Jean-Baptiste Bagaza.

The wave of violence began on Augst 14th and was directly related to the 1972 genocide against the Hutu. Hutus living in some parts of northern Burundi feared that the Tutsi were about to launch another campaign of terror to massacre them as they did in 1972. So, in a pre-emptive strike, they attacked the Tutsi and killed thousands of them. In the first week alone, one-fifteenth of the population of the provinces involved in the war were killed.

In retaliation, the Tutsi-dominated army massacred more than 20,000 Hutus, far in excess of the number of Tutsi victims, about 5,000 of whom were killed. Some reports show the death toll among the Hutu exceeded 25,000.[20]

Yet, all this happened under a leader who was considered to be relatively moderate and was reported to have ordered action only against armed rebels; a departure from the scorched-earth policy of indiscriminate killings of Hutus pursued by his predecessors through the years. And Burundi continued to face the lingering question: What should have been done to avoid this wave of violence that was only a part of the vicious cycle of terror and bloodshed that had been going on since the Belgians left after independence in 1962? How could the rest of the world have helped to end the violence?

One response came from the victims themselves, the Hutu. Living as refugees in neighbouring countries, they formed a militant organisation, the Hutu People's Liberation Party (PALIPEHUTU, its acronym in French, Burundi's official language), to fight for their rights.

The party was virulently anti-Tutsi as anyone can tell from its literature:

"Whether it's Micombero, Bagaza, or Buyoya, they all

come from the same hill and they are all Bahima [Tutsi]....It is this detestable race which had stolen from a huge number of Hutu since independence, and now all Tutsi are getting together to exterminate the Hutu."[21]

The Tutsi used the same kind of highly inflammatory language, thus precluding the possibility of any compromise or meaningful concessions and a negotiated settlement between the two sides to end this vicious cycle of violence.

The genocidal impulse that was evident among the Tutsi, as demonstrated by their massacre of Hutus in the past, was also clearly on display among the Hutu during their 1988 uprising in northern Burundi. They described the killings as their *gukora* (work), and *gutema* (cutting down) Tutsis as their patriotic duty in the service of the Hutu nation.

But even in this conflict, the Tutsi seemed to be determined to show that they had greater capacity to kill. They used heavy weapons to massacre Hutus at will, mowing them down even when they tried to flee. Many of them were shot in the back as they tried to flee to Rwanda, a massacre that was witnessed by UN observers on the border between the two countries. The Hutu refugees from Burundi were a constant reminder to their kinsmen in Rwanda of what would happen to them if the Tutsi ever came back to rule them again.

The fear was confirmed in the 1990s and thereafter when the Tutsi reconquered Rwanda and went on to retaliate against the Hutu for the massacre of their kinsmen in the 1994 genocide and continued to subjugate and kill the Hutu indiscriminately during the following years to perpetuate Tutsi domination of the country.

The ethnic conflict in Burundi prompted Buyoya in late 1988 to form a new government under a Hutu prime minister in an attempt to save Burundi from degenerating into chaos. The cabinet had equal numbers of Hutus and

175

Tutsis. He also promised to give Hutus more power. But it was not proportional allocation of power, 85 per cent of posts for Hutus, to reflect the percentage of the Hutu in the total population. Had Hutus been given that many posts, 85%, the Tutsi would not have accepted that.

It was, instead, an arrangement that left veto power in the hands of the Tutsi, with Buyoya himself dismissing the principle of majority rule when he said it was "an insult to democracy to confuse the democratic majority with the political majority."[22]

That is the same kind of subterfuge and twisted logic politically dominant minority groups – including whites in South Africa during the transition to majority rule in the early 1990s – have always used to try to perpetuate themselves in office as they retain veto power over the majority they have always oppressed and exploited. And that is a recipe for catastrophe as the history of Burundi itself, and even of Rwanda under Tutsi domination, tragically demonstrates.

The wave of violence that erupted in Burundi in October 1993 following the assassination of the country's first democratically elected president – Melchior Ndadaye, a Hutu – by Tutsi soldiers, and which claimed more than 200,000 lives, mostly Hutu, within the first three years, was only the latest in a series of tragedies that had befallen the embattled country since independence because of the Tutsis' determination to dominate the Hutu. Years later, the country was still embroiled in conflict which had already cost hundreds of thousands of lives.

Some analysts believe that the number of people killed in Burundi through the decades since independence exceeds the number of those who were killed in the Rwandan genocide in 1994. They were mostly Hutus killed by Tutsis who ruled the country since 1962.

In Rwanda, the Tutsis' hegemonic control of the country since 1994 when they seized power from the Hutu did little to reconcile the two sides let alone heal the wounds of genocide they themselves helped to start; not only by invading Rwanda from Uganda for the first time in October 1990 but also by triggering the genocide.

When the Tutsi invaded Rwanda in October 1990 with a force of about 7,000 fighters, they put the Hutu on the defensive and sent a wave of fear throughout the Hutu population, the majority of whom feared that their former oppressors were coming back to dominate them again and take their land and property.

The argument that it was the Tutsi themselves who triggered the genocide in which about one million of their own people perished is a highly sensitive subject among the Tutsi rulers of Rwanda. But there seems to be some evidence pointing in that direction, as various reports have shown through the years. Even as far back 2000, there were indications that Tutsi leaders played a role in triggering the genocide, even though there is no question that Hutus had been planning to exterminate the Tutsi for years since October 1990 when the Tutsi-dominated Rwandan Patriotic Army (RPA) first invaded Rwanda.

A UN memo leaked in March 2000 raised serious suspicions that it was Tutsi soldiers of the Rwandan Patriotic Army in a plot masterminded by Paul Kagame, and not the Hutu in the Rwandan national army as suspected earlier, who shot down the plane carrying Rwandan President Juvénal Habyarimana and his Burundian counterpart and fellow Hutu, President Cyprien Ntaryamira, thus triggering the massacre of their own people by enraged Hutus.

They shot down the plane, not anticipating massive retaliation by the Hutu against the Tutsi civilian population, because they had humiliated the Hutu-dominated national army – having fought it almost to a standstill and sometimes even outmanoeuvred it during the war – and felt that they were in an advantageous position to seize power and rule the country without a coalition government the two sides had agreed to form at their meeting in Tanzania.

The resignation of Rwandan Hutu President Pasteur Bizimungu on 23 March 2000 in protest against Tutsi domination of the government seemed to confirm that. And he was not the only Hutu high-ranking official to leave the Tutsi-dominated government. According to *The Christian Science Monitor*:

"The president who had ruled Rwanda since the genocide of 1994 resigned, becoming the latest in a series of high-ranking Hutus to leave the government this year....Reports said Bizimungu, a symbol of reconciliation between Hutus and the minority Tutsi population, had a 'falling out' with leaders of his own (Tutsi-dominated) Rwandan Patriotic Front, and especially with its Tutsi chairman, vice president Paul Kagame."[23]

And the leaked UN memo only seemed to confirm further that the Rwandan Patriotic Front (RPF) regime in Kigali wanted to consolidate and perpetuate Tutsi domination of the country. Many Hutus who left the coalition government – it was a coalition in name only – were forced to resign for a number of reasons including criticising the dominant Tutsi leadership and the unwillingness by Tutsi leaders to take their views into account when making important policy decisions.

In fact, one of the main reasons Bizimungu resigned was that he was not allowed to choose his own cabinet members freely,[24] the way he should been able to, as president, in spite of some restrictions on him in a government which was supposed to be run by collective leadership forging a consensus on decision making.

But even reaching such a consensus depended on the wishes of the dominant Tutsi leaders, especially Paul Kagame who, although vice president, was the most powerful man in the country.

A few days after President Bizimungu resigned, the

Rwandan Patriotic Front appointed Paul Kagame as president and said his term would end in 2003. Even before he became president, Kagame had enormous power. His position as *de facto* ruler of Rwanda was further strengthened by another cabinet post he held as defence minister.

Tragically, the resignation of President Bizimungu threatened to derail the peace process and could even, along with other resignations by senior Hutu officials, push the country to the brink of catastrophe including civil strife short of full-scale war between the Hutu and the Tutsi-dominated government. According to a report from Kigali, Rwanda, by *The Christian Science Monitor*:

"The coalition of 'unity' – made up of both Tutsis and moderate Hutus – that formed Rwanda's government following the country's 1994 genocide, appears to be crumbling.

Vice President Paul Kagame was appointed interim president, following the Thursday (March 23, 2000) resignation of President Pasteur Bizimungu....The Supreme Court of Rwanda appointed...Kagame as interim chief of state, rather than the expected choice, Parliament Speaker Vincent Biruta. The move appeared to pave the way for Kagame to win the post outright when parliament and the cabinet choose a new president, a process that must be completed within one month.

Kagame had previously been reluctant to assume the presidency so as not to antagonize Rwanda's Hutu majority, many of whom already believe that Tutsis control the country. Pasteur Bizimungu, a Hutu, resigned under pressure last week....

The resignation apparently resulted from clashes between Mr. Bizimungu, a moderate, and Mr. Kagame, whose Ugandan-based Tutsi-led guerrilla forces drove Hutu militants responsible for genocide out of Rwanda. Bizimungu's resignation comes just months after both the prime minister and the speaker of parliament quit their posts.

Political analysts count Bizimungu as the eighth Hutu to resign from an important post citing the impunity of a powerful Tutsi clique, and unfair reprisals and corruption witch hunts against prominent Hutus....

Independent observers say the resignations signal a deepening power struggle within Rwanda's government – raising questions about a regime that promised to bring stability, but is already under fire for fueling Africa's biggest war (in Congo). 'The final step of removing Bizimungu is the end of that hope of a multiethnic government,' says Alison Des Forges, consultant for Human Rights Watch and author of a book on the Rwandan genocide. She says Bizimungu was the last remaining Hutu in the inner circle of power.

Long seen as a figure-head, Bizimungu's resignation is unlikely to change much about the way things work in Rwanda. But the growing number of critics of Rwanda's ruling party say it spells out a pattern of undemocratic and sometimes violent power struggles within the Rwandan Patriotic Front (RPF) – as well as a move away from the hopeful national unity espoused in government rhetoric....

Rwanda has come under increasing fire for its role as a catalyst in Africa's 'great war' in the neighboring Democratic Republic of Congo....Now in control of an area in Congo 15 times its own size, Rwanda has earned an image as the region's feistiest power-broker. That image could turn sour, observers say, in the wake of a recent UN report accusing Rwanda of ignoring an arms embargo in Angola (arming UNITA rebels, instead) and new speculations – based on a leaked UN memo – that Kagame's own soldiers fired the fatal shot that broke a peace agreement and sparked the genocide."[25]

Compounding the problem is the fact that when in April 2000 Kagame became Rwanda's first Tutsi president

180

since the country won independence in July 1962, he was – after serving as interim president – confirmed in that post mostly by fellow Tutsis who dominated the coalition government. Hutu members who voted for him were no more than puppets manipulated at will by their Tutsi rulers. Therefore, their vote did not really count as a genuine endorsement of Kagame. Even if they voted against him, nobody would have taken them seriously. And they would have been marked men.

As the Tutsi continued to perpetuate themselves in office, it seemed that they had reduced the lessons from the 1994 holocaust to mere footnotes in the archives of Rwanda's history that is dominated by the struggle for power between the two ethnic groups which have the misfortune of living together, trapped within the same borders against their will, regardless of professions to the contrary by some members on both sides of the great divide.

The bloodshed in Rwanda and Burundi is essentially a product of power struggle, and land scarcity, between the Hutu and the Tutsi. But it is also a struggle rooted in and motivated by tribalism as clearly shown by the ethnic composition of political parties and other organisations. Each group to its own. And that is a continental phenomenon.

Denying the existence of tribalism in Rwanda and Burundi, and pretending that the two groups, Hutu and Tutsi, do not exist or no longer exist, is delusional. And it is not going to end the conflict between the two.

If Hutus and Tutsis don't exist – only Rwandans and Burudians do as some leaders claim – who is fighting who? And why do the people of the two countries identify themselves as Hutus or as Tutsis? It is true that they have intermingled and have intermarried for so long that the original groups no longer exist as "pure" biological units and with their own physical attributes. But they still do exist as social units even if not necessarily as biological entities each with its own separate gene pool and distinct physical features, although even today, there are some physical differences between Hutus and Tutsis but not all.

And they will continue to compete for power as long as they see themselves as distinct groups, each with its own interests and loyalties, a phenomenon not peculiar to Rwanda and Burundi.

More often than not, the struggle for power in most African countries is shaped by ethno-regional interests and loyalties. It is inexorably linked to tribalism because almost all African countries are no more than patchwork quilts of different ethnic groups hardly united by a common identity besides the national flag and the same passport. All these groups have their own prejudices. They have conflicting interests. They distrust each other and even hate each other, although not in all cases. And their ethnic loyalties transcend nationalism and Pan-Africanism – that's what tribalism is all about – making it very difficult to achieve national unity, especially when some tribes dominate others.

Although tribalism bedevils every African country, only in varying degrees, Rwanda and Burundi are some of the countries which have suffered the most from tribal conflicts, a scourge that goes on unabated in both countries, exacerbated by Tutsis ensconced in power.

The Belgian colonial rulers compounded the tragedy when they anointed the Tutsi as the natural rulers of the Hutu, thus legitimising and perpetuating the feudalistic institutions established by the Tutsi to institutionalise their supremacy and the asymmetrical relationship – inequality of power and so on – between the two groups.

Like other colonial rulers across Africa, the Belgians also exploited old antagonisms and ethnic differences between the Hutu and the Tutsi to facilitate imperial rule – as much as they did in the Belgian Congo – thereby exacerbating ethnic tensions and creating new ones where they did not exist; for example, between some Hutus and

Tutsi commoners, especially in Burundi which was less stratified than Rwanda.

The Hutu and Tutsi commoners in Burundi collectively constituted a subordinate group as opposed to the Tutsi princes, the *ganwa*, who showed characteristics of a group evolving into a caste, even different from fellow Tutsis not just Hutus. But the evolution into a caste system – a rigidly stratified society – was never completed in Burundi as it was in Rwanda where almost all Hutus constituted the "wretched heap" at the bottom with the Tutsi sitting on top. Yet, in both countries, the Belgians played the race card, Tutsi versus Hutu and vice versa and, by doing so, helped to put the two countries on a blood-soaked path towards self destruction along ethnic lines instead of building genuinely pluralistic societies on the basis of a national consensus.

Therefore, the Belgian colonial rulers had the opportunity to help contain ethnic rivalry and hostility and minimise its impact on political developments in both Rwanda and Burundi by preparing the two countries for independence on a genuinely democratic basis through accommodation of conflicting ethnic interests and loyalties on the basis of peaceful co-existence. This could have been achieved by creating new power structures on ethnic basis to guarantee security and equality for all instead of leaving the Tutsi on top; and by decentralising power all the way down to the grassroots level to make the central government less attractive to aspiring dictators and tribalists.

If the centralised state had been stripped of most of its powers by creating multiple centres of power, it would have been virtually impossible for any group to organise let alone execute a military coup or dominate the other and perpetuate itself in power. The multiple centres of power would have constituted a very strong system of checks and balances – and a powerful disincentive – to prevent the emergence of autocracy and neither the Hutu nor the Tutsi would have been able to dominate either country: Rwanda or Burundi.

Had the Belgians restructured Rwanda and Burundi on an egalitarian basis, the oppressed Hutu majority would have welcomed and embraced the change. The only people who would have been opposed to that would have been the Tutsi because they were on top and would not have liked losing their power and privileges in a genuinely pluralistic society run on democratic basis. Yet, peace and stability in Rwanda and Burundi demanded such sacrifice on their part (the Tutsi) which, unfortunately, they were not willing to make. Therefore the Belgians as the colonial rulers should have compelled them to do so at least 10 years before independence and the tragedy that befell the two countries would probably have been avoided.

Nigeria also comes to mind for comparative study and analysis in this context. Had the British listened to Nigerian leaders such as Nnamdi Azikiwe and Chief Obafemi Awolowo who demanded in the 1940s and 1950s the creation of more states – on ethnic and cultural-linguistic basis to accommodate the interests of all the 250 or so ethnic groups, which would have been a form of decentralisation in that giant African colony – to replace the three massive regions dominated by only three ethnic groups (the Hausa-Fulani in the North, the Yoruba in the West, and the Igbo in the East) at the expense of others, Nigeria would have emerged from colonial rule as a stable federation and ready for true democracy.

And it probably would have avoided the civil war that almost destroyed the country during the turbulent sixties when the Igbo and other Eastern Nigerians seceded from the federation and proclaimed independence for Eastern Nigeria as the Republic of Biafra to avoid oppression and more massacres – after more than 30,000 Easterners, mostly Igbo, were massacred in Northern Nigeria – by the Hausa-Fulani who dominated the Nigerian federation as the Tutsi did in Rwanda and Burundi at the expense of the

Hutu majority.

In both cases, Nigeria and Ruanda-Urundi, colonial rule should probably have lasted longer than it did, may be for another three to five years or may be even a little longer than that depending on local circumstances, in order to reorganise and restructure those countries. For example, it would have depended on how stable or unstable the political situation was in those colonial territories.

But that is the price Africans should have been prepared to pay for the future stability of their countries, Nigeria, Rwanda and Burundi being only three examples. Other prime candidates would have been the Belgian Congo and Sudan.

There is no question that if the new states, regions, provinces or other administrative structures were to be created on an egalitarian basis before independence, they would have needed some time to settle down in order to be able to function smoothly as integral parts of collective entities (African nations) after the end of colonial rule. Nowhere is this missed opportunity more apparent, and its consequences so devastating, than in Rwanda, Burundi, Nigeria, the former Belgian Congo and Sudan.

In the case of Rwanda and Burundi, which is the focus of this study, something can still be done to end the perennial conflict in those two countries in the green hills of Africa which have had the unenviable distinction of being some of the worst killing fields in the world.

With regard to Rwanda, the resignation of President Pasteur Bizimungu – after almost six years in office (July 1994 – March 2000) – in protest against the Tutsis' hegemonic control of the country underscored the imperative need for dynamic compromise and other bold initiatives to resolve the conflict between the Hutu and the Tutsi. Such compromise is also the only viable solution in the case of Burundi.

Both sides, the Hutu and the Tutsi, must be willing to

make enormous concessions and sacrifices to achieve lasting peace and stability.

At the core of the problem is insecurity of the Tutsi minority, not simply their desire to dominate the Hutu. They are afraid of majority rule because they think it will lead to oppression or even to their extermination under Hutu-dominated governments as happened in Rwanda in 1994. And it is very difficult for them to be convinced otherwise after what happened in Rwanda.

Therefore the Hutu in both countries must make concessions which will make the Tutsi secure. For the concessions to be meaningful, the Tutsi themselves *must* also *feel* secure. They must believe that they are secure and that they are guaranteed security by the Hutu majority.

But the Tutsi also must recognise the imperative need for the Hutu to be accorded their rights as the majority in the population of both countries.

Yet democracy in Rwanda and Burundi can not be based on the principle of majority rule alone. If it is, the Tutsi will be swamped. They are vastly outnumbered by the Hutu. Therefore a formula must be found under which the Tutsi will also enjoy democracy as a minority but without compromising the rights of the Hutu majority.

Genuine proportional representation may be one way to achieve this goal. Another way is self-rule in separate autonomous ethnic entities – Hutu and Tutsi – which can be created to provide security for members of the two groups separately.

The autonomous ethnic entities can also act as a counterweight against the central government which may be dominated by one group or the other or which may try to ignore the demands and interests of the people at the local or grassroots level. The autonomous entities can constitute clusters of self-governing communities with their own governments vested with a lot of power to manage their own affairs without getting orders or directives from the national government.

And it is the representatives of these self-governing communities who should form the national government, not just any individuals chosen by the president.

The government itself should govern on the basis of consensus in a country which can be transformed into a confederation of autonomous ethnic entities.

Rule by consensus is vital to allay fears among the Tutsi who are a minority in both countries. If the Tutsi feel that they are not adequately represented and their interests are ignored, there will be no peace in Rwanda and Burundi.

It is easier for the Hutu majority to deal with insecurity than it is for the Tutsi minority who fear they will be swamped and exterminated by the Hutu majority if they are ignored.

Since the Hutu constitute a formidable majority, they know there is security in numbers. It is impossible for the Tutsi to wipe out the Hutu. But it is easy for the Hutu to exterminate the Tutsi if they decide to do so. And it is impossible to convince the Tutsi that the Hutu won't try that or won't do it again as they did in Rwanda in 1994. The Rwandan genocide will always be on their mind.

Other countries across the continent torn by civil conflicts may be compelled to seek radical solutions to their problems. The solutions may entail creative destruction, a subject addressed in the last part of the book.

Conclusion

Rwanda and Burundi:
The Road Not Taken

THIS STUDY has focused on the political and ethnic conflicts in Rwanda and Burundi. By doing so, it has also addressed the subject of conflict resolution in Africa even if in the limited context of the two countries and the Great Lakes region of East Africa. But it serves as a case study applicable in other contexts as well, in Africa, and is therefore continental in scope in terms of relevance.

I have concluded the study with an inquiry into what can be done to end conflicts in the two East African countries whose fate is inexorably linked with the destiny of the entire Great Lakes region of which they are an integral part. The destiny of the region itself is, of course, linked with the destiny of the entire continent. As Sekou Toure once said, African is like the human body. When one finger is cut, the whole body feels the pain.

The fundamental question facing Rwanda and Burundi is not whether the Hutu and the Tutsi can live together. They can, as they have during the past 400 years or so. The fundamental question is whether or not they want to live together.

Do they really want to live together or are they forced by their leaders to do so?

If they don't want to live together, what should they do besides trying to exterminate each other or dominate one another?

Neither the Hutu nor the Tutsi themselves have fully answered these questions.

An honest answer to the first question is inhibited by fear of fragmentation: break up one African country, expect others to follow suit. Therefore maintain territorial integrity by any means, at any cost, even if it means forcing tribes which are enemies to live together and to work together regardless of how much they hate each other and kill each other, making cooperation of any kind almost impossible.

The answer to the second question – what should they do if they don't want to live together? – is related to the first and is also inhibited by fear of fragmentation but also by petty and retrogressive nationalism: the unwillingness of African countries to open their borders and take in fellow Africans who want to settle in those countries or move freely across borders.

Such a policy, of liberal migration and free movement of people across borders, will help a lot to facilitate regional integration and promote African unity.

We should remember that before the partition of Africa and the advent of colonial rule, Africans migrated freely. They settled in other parts of Africa without hindrance and without being told to go back where they came from. In my home country, Tanzania, there are people who migrated all the way from South Africa. They are the

Ngoni. They migrated from Natal Province and settled in what is now Ruvuma Region in southern Tanzania in the 1840s. Other Ngonis settled in other parts of Tanzania during the same period. Some of them migrated to Congo. They moved freely. They did not have to get permission to cross borders. There were no borders until Europeans came.

The Maasai and the Luo migrated from Sudan about 300 years ago and settled in the areas that became the countries of Kenya and Tanzania. The Ga migrated from Nigeria to Ghana; the Baoule from Ghana to the Ivory Coast; the Ndebele from South Africa to Zimbabwe. The list goes on and on.

All those people were able to move freely and settle in the areas where they wanted to settle because we did not have restrictive borders before we were colonised. After our European conquerors partitioned the continent, we became different people instead of being just Africans. The boundaries they drew defined us. We became Tanganyikans, Kenyans, Nigerians, Gambians, Ugandans and so on.

Some of the ethnic conflicts we have in Africa can be resolved by opening up our borders and allowing the people to migrate freely and settle in other countries. For example, within my home region of East Africa, some Tutsis migrated from Rwanda and settled in eastern Congo where they came to be known as Banyamulenge.

After the Rwandan genocide, hundreds of thousands of Hutus sought refuge in eastern Congo. Many of them still live there. And through the decades, hundreds of thousands of people, Hutus and Tutsis from Rwanda and Burundi, and many other people of different ethnic groups from Congo have sought refuge in Tanzania. Tens of thousands have become citizens through the years. Refugees from Mozambique have also lived in Tanzania for decades. Many of them also have become citizens.

All those people crossed borders without affecting the

territorial integrity of the countries which took them in. There was plenty of land for them. They took none from the citizens of those countries.

Open the borders – and even abolish them – so that our people can migrate and settle freely in other countries. Julius Nyerere once suggested that because there is not enough land in Rwanda and Burundi, neighbouring countries should open their borders to allow the Hutu and the Tutsi to migrate to those countries in order to defuse tensions and conflict between the two groups in their homelands.

The conflict between the two is over power: who is in power and who should be in power, one or the other. It also revolves around the land question which is also inextricably linked with who is in power and who is not: Hutu or Tutsi.

There is also another solution that is not openly discussed, although it has been discussed privately by African leaders through the years: partition.

Kenyan President Daniel arap Moi is one of the few African leaders who have mentioned this publicly, as he did at a press conference in Nairobi in April 1998. He said the Hutu and the Tutsi should be separated. The Hutu should have their country, and the Tutsi also should have their own country in order to end conflicts between them.

Africans and other people including UN officials should openly discuss the partition of Rwanda and Burundi into independent ethnostates. Separation may not end hatred between the two groups. And it may not end dictatorship – there will always be aspiring dictators among the Hutu even in Hutuland and among the Tutsi in Tutsiland – if Rwanda and Burundi were to partitioned along ethnic lines. But it will end the bloodshed between them and save hundreds of thousands – if not millions – of lives which could be lost in conflicts between the two groups.

Separation of the two groups also has other advantages

besides providing each one of them with its own homeland where its members can live in peace and security without fear of oppression and domination, persecution and extermination, by the other group. It will also solve the refugee problem which is such a burden on the refugees themselves and on the neighbouring countries – especially Tanzania and Congo – and on the international community. Only the partition of Rwanda and Burundi will enable the refugees to return home freely (to Hutuland or Tutsiland) and in security if they are not going to be absorbed by their host countries.

Therefore, there is a way to end their misery as refugees and as victims of ethnocide at home, besides trying to form coalition governments and establish democracy in a pluralistic context; knowing full well that such solutions are not going to work in the case of Rwanda and Burundi on long-term basis, except temporarily although even that is not a guarantee.

Coalition governments have not worked. They have failed repeatedly in both Rwanda and Burundi. And democracy means only one thing in this context of combustible elements. The Hutu who constitute the vast majority of the population in both countries will rule forever. They will never lose an election to the Tutsi on the basis of one man, one vote. And no Tutsi in his or her right mind is going to accept that. Put yourself in their position.

It is equally true for the Hutu. No Hutu is going to accept anything short of true democracy, to which the Hutu are entitled since they are the majority and therefore entitled to form a government in accordance with the fundamental principle of democracy: majority rule.

They are not going to accept anything short of that for the same reason blacks and other non-whites in South Africa – after more than 350 years of racial oppression by whites – refused to give up their democratic rights under a system of power sharing with whites which would have given whites veto power on any decisions and policy matters. Their status as the majority group would have been meaningless because of the veto power exercised by the white minority.

Democracy has, of course, been established in South Africa. But that is because whites – the former rulers – have, although reluctantly, accepted black majority rule as a fact of life. They can't do anything to change that besides leaving the country if they don't want to live under a predominantly black government, a decision many of them have made, migrating mostly to countries which are mostly white.

Tens of thousands of whites have left South Africa through the years since 1994 when the first democratically elected multiracial government in the nation's history was established under the leadership of Nelson Mandela. They have left willingly – blacks have not asked or forced them to leave – and have found countries which are ready to accept them, especially Australia, New Zealand, the United States, Canada, and Britain.

That is not the case with the Tutsi in Rwanda and Burundi. For them to accept democracy or majority rule is suicidal. As a minority who also had been the rulers of both Rwanda and Burundi for centuries, the Tutsi are in a position similar to that of the white minority in South Africa. But the similarity ends there.

It is true that the Hutu and the Tutsi can also have democracy in Rwanda and Burundi. But that is only if the Tutsi are going to accept majority rule on the basis of one man, one vote (not on the basis of one Tutsi, three or five votes and so on).

If they accept that, it automatically means a predominantly Hutu government, and a predominantly Hutu parliament, a dreadful prospect for the minority group who already are not on very good terms with the country's majority.

Therefore to them, partition is probably an attractive proposition for their own safety, if that is the only alternative to Hutu majority rule, besides continuing bloodshed under the presented circumstances of forced amalgamation of the two ethnic groups within the same national boundaries under the same jurisdiction of the highly centralised state so typical of so many African countries.

Separation of the Hutu and the Tutsi into independent states has yet another advantage. There will be no need for any peacekeeping forces which are not easy to get in the first place as the 1994 Rwandan genocide tragically demonstrated. The two groups will be living separate lives. Therefore there will be no need for any kind of intervention to stop or resolve ethnic conflicts within the borders. Each group will have its own country.

Partition may not be the best solution. But in some cases, it is the only solution as is the case between the Israelis and the Palestinians; so it is in the case of the Hutu and the Tutsi.

It is also true that as a tool in conflict resolution, partition has some disadvantages, besides its advantages. In the African context especially, where the quest for unity is a perennial quest and ambition of many Africans including ordinary people and not just leaders, partition impedes progress towards achieving the goal of unity: Africans working together, uniting and even forming governments on regional basis after uniting several countries here and there under one leadership.

Separation of warring tribes or ethnic groups into independent ethnostate also disrupts established ties which cut across ethnic lines. There are many communities where members of different tribes live together in harmony in every African country, including those torn by ethnic conflicts. And they have lived that way for years, in some cases for centuries. Many have even intermarried for generations or for centuries. They include the Hutu and the Tutsi in both Rwanda and Burundi, although they turned against each other during the 1994 Rwandan holocaust,

Hutus killing their Tutsi relatives, friends and neighbours, with some Tutsis also retaliating but mostly in self-defence, if they could; in most cases, they were defenceless..

Not all of Hutus turned against their relatives. But a large number of them did, probably even more so against their friends.

Yet that does not mean all tribes which fight or don't like each other should be separated; nor does such hostility justify breaking up multiethnic societies, whether they are integrated or not, although, for example, the Igbo and other Easterners in Nigeria were justified in seceding after their fellow countrymen in Northern Nigeria turned against them and the regional government in the north and the federal government itself did nothing to protect them and stop the massacres, forcing them to flee to their homeland where they declared independence as the Republic of Biafra.

So, there are exceptions where separation or secession is justified even if means taking a step backwards in Africa's long march towards unity.

But that does not mean we should ignore the negative aspects of separation even when it helps to end some conflicts. Besides what has already been pointed out, separation also violates individual rights. People should be able to live where they want to live. Also, they should be able to live with whom they want to live and marry whom they want to marry. It is their right, not the state's. Partition of countries into ethnostates violates this fundamental right.

It also leads to ethnic cleansing, forcing members of "alien" groups trapped behind new borders to leave their homes and move to the place "where they belong." Thus, Hutus will have to leave the newly created sovereign Tutsi state which has been established exclusively for the Tutsi, and move to Hutuland, or risk their lives – and probably get killed right away – if they insist on remaining on enemy territory. Like the Hutu, the Tutsi will be forced to do the same thing, breaking up many families.

Tragically, in the case of both Rwanda and Burundi, each group is already on enemy territory, trapped. It is shared territory. It belongs to both. The Hutu and the Tutsi claim the same areas as theirs and in many cases even share and live on the same piece of land. And their fate is inextricably linked by culture, by history, and even by family ties, thus making separation of the two groups infinitely difficult to achieve.

But, just as they are able to move in large numbers when they are fleeing as refugees, they can also move *en masse* if they want to establish independent ethnostates and live in peace with their own kind separate from their enemies. Without separation, they are left with the ghastly alternative: endless civil wars, oppression or extermination of the weaker group. Given these choices, those who oppose partition, sanction oppression and genocide in the name of brotherhood.

If the Hutu and the Tutsi can not separate and establish independent ethnostates of Hutuland and Tutsiland in both Rwanda and Burundi, hundreds of thousands and may be even millions – in order to ease population pressures – should be allowed to migrate to other African countries where they should be allowed to settle, not as exiles or mere guests but as citizens they same way they have been given citizenship in Tanzania and other countries through the years.

African countries should also redefine and enlarge their concept of citizenship to make it Pan-African in scope even if it is in a limited regional context. The people in East African countries should have a common East African citizenship and should travel on the same passport as East African citizens, thus enabling them to move freely across borders and live in any country they want to live in to facilitate integration. West Africans also should have a common West African citizenship. The people in the countries of southern Africa should also be accorded the same status in their region, as should those in the central African countries and in North Africa.

Eventually, they all should have the same citizenship on a continental scale and travel on the same Pan-African passport. But before taking such a quantum leap to continental citizenship as is the case in the European Union in some respects, African countries must first build trust and cooperation among themselves at the regional level by granting common citizenship to all their citizens.

Such regional citizenship will be a major step towards African unity. It will also spread the burden of refugees to all the countries in the subcontinental region – East, West, Central, North, and South – instead of expecting only one country or two or none to handle the burden. For example, in East Africa, more than 200,000 Rwandan and Burundian refugees have been granted Tanzanian citizenship through the decades since the sixties, especially since the seventies. More than 80,000 were granted citizenship in the early 1980s alone.

But Tanzania can't absorb all the refugees all the time. Therefore other countries in the region and beyond should also welcome them as citizens, taking in large numbers of them. After the 1994 genocide, some Hutus who fled Rwanda after the Tutsi seized power and became the new rulers said they were ready to walk all the way to West Africa where they originally came from, a historical connection they were obviously aware of, since the members of all the other ethnic groups in East, Central and Southern Africa who belong to the Bantu linguistic group migrated from what is now Cameroon and east-central Nigeria.

Many of them walked all the way to Congo-Brazzaville and other countries.

Spreading out refugees and taking in large numbers of them across the continent will also greatly reduce conflicts over land in Rwanda and Burundi which are the most densely populated countries in Africa; they are also some of the smallest. It will also ease ethnic tensions between the Hutu and the Tutsi and probably even end some hostilities which have claimed more than 2 million lives in both countries since the 1970s alone.

And even if the two countries are split along ethnic lines into independent ethnostates of Hutuland and Tutsiland, with the help of the international community if possible, including financial inducements, such sepapration does not have to be absolute. The two ethnic groups, out of necessity and not necessarily out of love for each other, can still work together in a number of areas of common interest for their own wellbeing. They can't avoid being neighbours. Even the most bitter enemies can live in peaceful coexistence for mutual benefit. Such cooperation, especially in the economic arena, can help establish and strengthen regional ties and integrate the new nations – created out of Rwanda and Burundi – with their neighbours to create a cohesive regional bloc.

Short of partition, Rwanda and Burundi can pursue unity in diversity, opening the way towards genuine power sharing on the basis of proportional representation in a confederation of autonomous ethnic enclaves, making it impossible for one ethnic group to dominate the other within the same national boundaries.

Strip the central government of most of its powers under whose jurisdiction both the Hutu and the Tutsi have perpetrated some of the worst atrocities against each other in the name of equality and justice. Let the people decide and rulc themselves at the local level, with the central or national government playing only a limited role in terms of governance.

Ethnic pogroms have earned the two East African countries the unenviable distinction as the killing fields of Africa. There have been other massacres and wars of comparable magnitude elsewhere on the continent. But nowhere, except in Sudan, and in Nigeria during its civil war in the late sixties, has the violence assumed monstrous ethnic dimensions and has been carried out with such ferocity as in Rwanda and Burundi.

Yet, it is from these same countries that a final solution to some of Africa's bloodiest conflicts may emerge, entailing creative destruction – partition of Rwanda and Burundi along ethnic lines – for the sake of unity.

Only then will the two blood-soaked countries embark on the road towards peace – may be even reconciliation between the Hutu and the Tutsi – and rightfully claim their well-deserved reputation as the green hills of Africa, no longer soaked with the blood of the enemy who happens to be a fellow countryman, yet a stranger in his own homeland. And only then will they give concrete expression to the words of the anthem of the Organisation of African Unity (OAU) which have yet to ring true across this embattled continent:

> Oh sons and daughters of Africa
> Flesh of the sun and flesh of the sky
> Let us make Africa the tree of life
> Let us all unite and toil together
> To give the best we have to Africa
> The cradle of mankind and fount of culture.

Notes

Part One:

1. "Hutu Rebels Terrorize 3 Nations: The Slaughter Continues – It's a Regional Problem," *International Herald Tribune*, January 29, 1998, p. 2; *The Washington Post*, January 29, 1998.

2. Seth Kamanzi, ibid.

3. Ibid. See also "Crackdown on Burundi Rebels Forces 350,000 Hutu into Camps," *International Herald Tribune*, December 28, 1999, pp. 1, and 4; "The Recent Roots of Hutu-Tutsi Hate," *International Herald Tribune*, January 4, 2000, p. 7; "Burundi: Old War, New Mediator – Nelson Mandela Is to Mediate in Burundi's War, But Civilians Remain Trapped Between Rebel and Army Brutality," *The Economist*, January 22, 2000, pp. 46, and 4.

4. Alison DesForges, quoted in "Hutu Rebels Terrorize 3 Nations," op.cit.

5. Neil J. Kressel, *Mass Hate: The Global Rise of Genocide and Terror* (New York: Plenum Press), p. 115. See also Alain Destexhe, *Rwanda and Genocide in the Twentieth Century* (New York: New York University Press, 1995).

6. Paula Ghedini, quoted in Hutu Rebels Terrorize 3 Nations," op. cit.

7. Ibid.

8. International relief agency official, quoted ibid.

9. Seth Sendashonga, ibid.

10. "Hutu Rebels Terrorize 3 Nations," ibid.

11. Ibid. See also, "Rwanda: Continued Attacks," and "Burundi: Rebel Attacks Near Capital," in *Keesing's Record of World Events*, January 1998, p. 41991:

"Hutu militia attacks in western and central Rwanda continued throughout January, and a number of people of both Tutsi and Hutu origin were killed. At least five nuns died on January 8 in an attack on their convent near the north-western town of Gisenyi, which had been a focus for much of the violence.

The Rwandan News Agency reported that some 10,000 people had held a demonstration in Gisenyi on January 21 to protest against the ongoing violence, following a recent attack on a bus in which at least 35 had been killed....

In the first rebel assault for two years on a target near the capital (Bujumbura of Burundi), an estimated 1,000 Hutu rebels belonging to the armed wing of the National Council for the Defence of Democracy (CNDD) attacked a military camp and village close to Bujumbura airport on January 1. At least 284 people were reported to have been killed in the attack, among them many Hutu civilians from the village of Rukaramu.

Further rebel attacks on the outskirts of Bujumbura continued throughout January. The main road to the centre and north of the country was temporarily closed on January 11 following skirmishes in its vicinity. Some 42 rebels were reportedly killed at Isale, 10 kilometres from Bujumbura, on January 14, whilst on January 18 rebels targeted a military post at Gikongo, on the northern outskirts of the capital. Despite claims by military sources that the rebels had been repulsed, further exchanges of gunfire to the south of Bujumbura were reported on January 22." See also *Keesing's Record of World Events*, January 1998, pp. 41947, 41897, and 41851.

12. "Remembering A Slaughter: Rwandans Memorialize Tutsi Victims Who Fought Back," *The Boston Globe*, April 8, 1998, p. A-14.

13. Ibid.

14. "Two Priests Sentenced to Death in Rwanda Massacre," *The Boston Globe*, April 19, 1998, p. A-19.

15. Ibid.

16. Faustin Nteziryayo, quoted in "20 Prisoners to be Executed for Genocide of the Tutsi," *International Herald Tribune*, April 23, 1998, p. 4.

17. Radio Rwanda, quoting a cabinet communique, ibid.

18. Association of Peace Volunteers, survivors of the 1994 genocide, quoted, ibid. See also *The Christian Science Monitor*, April 23, 1998, p. 2.

19. Gideon Kayinamura, quoted in "Rwanda Says 20 Face Execution for War Crimes," *The Boston Globe*, April 23, 1998, p. A-2.

20. Peter Takirambudde, ibid.

21. Jose Luis Herrero, ibid.

22. Patrick Mazimhaka, in "Rwanda Firm on Execution of 22: No Clemency for Those Involved in Massacre of Tutsi," *The Boston Globe*, April 24, 1998, p. A-4.

23. Mary Robinson, ibid.

24. P. Mazimhaka, ibid.

25. "Rwanda Executes 22 As Genocide Planners: Thousands Applaud as Some Organizers of Massacres in 1994 Are Shot to Death," *International Herald Tribune*, April 25, 1998, pp. 1, and 7; *The Washington Post*, April 25, 1998.

26. "Rwanda Executes 22 for Genocide: Crowds Watch and Cheer," *The Boston Globe*, April 25, 1998, p. A-1.

27. Ibid.

28. Christine Mukarumongi, ibid., p. A-6.

29. Kato Ninyetegeka, ibid.

30. "22 Rwandans Executed for Roles in Genocide as Thousands Cheer," ibid., p. A-6; "In Rwanda, Blood Begets Blood: As Crowds Watch, the AK-47s Are Turned on Those Convicted of Leading the 1994 Massacres," *The Washington Post*, National Weekly Edition, May 4, 1998, pp. 17 – 18.

31. Rwandan official, who remained anonymous, quoted in "Executions Producing Confessions, Rwanda Says," *The Boston Globe*, April 26, 1998, p. A-21.

32. A senior official in the prosecutor's office in Kigali, ibid.

33. Alphonse Nteziryayo, *The Christian Science Monitor*, April 29, 1998, p. 2.

34. "Rural Rwanda's Catastrophes Give Rise to an AIDS Epidemic," *International Herald Tribune*, May 30, 1998, p. 2.

35. Ibid.

36. Pascale Crussard, ibid.

37. Eulerie Mukarugambwa, ibid.

38. Anastase Gasana, quoted in "Rwanda Denies Role in Killing," *International Herald Tribune*, May 19, 1998, p. 8.

39. "Civilians Slain in Rampage: Hundreds Killed by Rwanda Hutu," *The Boston Globe*, May 29, 1998, p. A-2.

40. Ibid.

41. Geoffrey Gatera, in *The Economist*, June 6, 1998, p. 8.

42. "UN to Pull Out Rights Mission from Rwanda: Government Talks Reach Impasse – In May, the Rwandan Government Suspended the Mandate of the Mission, Saying it Overemphasized Alleged Reprisal Killings," *The Boston Globe*, July 17, 1998, p. A-2.

43. *The Economist*, July 18, 1998, p. 6.

44. "Rwandans Sentenced to Death in Genocide," *International Herald Tribune*, July 20, 1998, p. 7.

45. "Two Missionaries Seized in Rwanda," *The Boston Globe*, July 23, 1998, p. A-20.

46. "Hutu Rebels Blamed in Hacking Deaths of 110 Rwandans," *The Boston Globe*, August 3, 1998, p. A-4; *International Herald Tribune*, August 3, 1998, p. 7; *The New York Times*, August 3, 1998; *Current History: A Journal of Contemporary World Affairs*, October 1998, p. 350.

47. "Hutu Rebels Storm Rwanda Jail, Free Inmates Held in '94 Killings," *The Boston Globe*, September 6, 1998, p. A-28.

48. Faustin Nzelilyayo (sic), cited in "Rwanda Plans to Free 10,000 Held in Genocide," *The Boston Globe*, October 10, 1998, p. A-6.

49. Paul Kagame, in "An African Survivor Now Faces Fight for Security: Interview (with) Paul Kagame – The Rwandan Leader Behind Three Invasions May Launch New Bid to Redraw Map of Congo," *The Christian Science Monitor*, October 13, 1998, p. 6.

50. Rwanda, in *Current History: A Journal of Contemporary World Affairs*, September 1998, p. 298; *Current History*, October 1998, p. 350. See also Philip Gourevitch, *We Wish to Inform You That Tomorrow We Will be Killed With Our Families: Stories From Rwanda* (New York: Farrar, Straus & Giroux, 1998); George Packer, "Rwanda's Machete Rule," *The Nation*, New York, November 16, 1998, pp. 58, 60, 61, and 62; Cameron W. Barr, "The Horrors of Looking Away From Rwanda," *The Christian Science Monitor*, February 4, 1999, p. 20.

51. *The Economist*, October 17, 1998, p. 4.

52. "Burundi Interns Hutu in Camps: Farmers Become The Victims of Crackdown on Guerrillas," *International Herald Tribune*, August 14, 1997, p. 2; "Crackdown on Burundi Rebels Forces 350,000 Hutu into Camps," *International Herald Tribune*, December 28, 1999, pp. 1, and 4.

53. "Rwanda's Enforced Villages: Now for Some Imugudusisation," *The Economist*, January 23, 1999, p. 43.

54. Ibid.

55. Diplomat in Kigali, Rwanda, who spoke on condition of anonymity, quoted, ibid. See also "Africa's Border-Breaching Conflict: Long Shadow of Sudden Tragedy," *The Christian Science Monitor*, March 9, 1999, p. 6:

"The Hutu make up 85 percent of Rwanda's population but have become increasingly marginalized by the Tutsi elite currently in power. They are largely excluded from political power and confined to their fields in rural areas.

In the northwestern prefectures of Ruhengeri and Gisenyi, Hutu civilians have been the target of often brutal military raids to flush out the Interahamwe. Human rights groups say the Rwandan Army has consistently failed to discriminate between rebels and civilians....

Observers believe that the solution to the Interahamwe problem lies partly with the government of Rwanda. 'The government has...become more exclusionary....I don't see a solution in what they are doing,' says Barnett Rubin, director of peace and conflict studies at the Council on Foreign Relations in New York."

See also "Hutu Problem Remains Intractable: Murders in Uganda Underscore Africa's and World's Ongoing Failure," *International Herald Tribune*, March 12, 1999, p. II:

"The massacre of foreign tourists in Uganda by Congo-based Rwandan rebels last week highlighted one of Central Africa's most intractable issues: how to reign in the Hutu extremists who have spread havoc across the region since their failed attempt to exterminate Rwanda's Tutsi minority in 1994....

Ugandan and Rwandan troops have been trying for years to vanquish the Hutu extremists....Yet, the Hutu diaspora still shakes Central Africa....Hutu extremists and numerous other stateless rebel groups...function like nomadic warriors and use eastern Congo...as a base. Of several Hutu groups scattered around Rwanda's borders, the Interahamwe – 'those who work together' in the Kinyarwanda language – is the most infamous. In Rwanda, before the Hutu were driven from power in 1994, the Interahamwe was a militia of about 50,000 members that coalesced around ethnic hatred. Today, fear of the exiled Interahamwe is so pervasive in the region that any Hutu with a weapon often is assumed to be a member.

The Interahamwe is allied with Hutu extremists who were members of Rwanda's Army, as well as with Congolese Hutu driven by similar ethnic animus. The group that killed the tourists in Uganda was identified as the Army for the Liberation of Rwanda, which a U.S. official said is closely linked to the Interahamwe."

See also Lynne Duke, on Rwanda, in *The Washington Post*, March 12, 1999; "Gorillas and Guerrillas," *The Washington Post*, National Weekly Edition, March 15, 1999, p. 25; "Massacre in the Mist: Africa's Implacable Hatreds Claim More Innocent Lives," *U.S. News & World Report*, March 15, 1999, pp. 35, 36, and 40: "Marauders in Africa's innumerable civil wars (include) some 20 rebel groups...in dense terrain in Rwanda, Uganda, and Congo (formerly Zaire), where (they) roam and plunder....A large swath of the continent has burst into flames."

56. "Hopes for Democracy As Rwandans Vote," *International Herald Tribune*, March 30, 1999, p. 7.

57. "Rwanda's Small But Crucial Election: Neither Hutu nor Tutsi, Just Rwandan," *The Economist*, April 3, 1999, p. 37.

58. Ibid.

59. "Hutu and Tutsi Ask: Is A Unified Rwanda Possible?," *The New York Times*, April 6, 1999, p. A-3.

60. Ibid.

61. Ibid.

62. "Bishop Seized by Rwanda in Massacres," *The New York Times*, April 15,1999, p. A-11.

63. "Honoring Victims of the Rwandan Blood Bath," *The New York Times*, April 8, 1999, p. A-3; René Lemarchand, "The Fire in the Great Lakes," *Current History: A Journal of Contemporary World Affairs*," May 1999, p. 196:

"Although the magnitude of the Rwandan holocaust is without precedent – it is estimated to have caused the deaths of a million people – the killing of tens of thousands of Hutu refugees at the hands of the Rwandan Patriotic Front Army (RPA, the armed wing of the RPF government), in eastern Congo in 1996 and 1997, can be considered a third genocide. And to this might be added the Kibeho killings, perpetrated inside Rwanda in April 1995, when at least 5,000 Hutu refugees were killed in cold blood by RPA units." See also *Current History*, ibid., pp. 195 – 201; Marina Ottaway, "Post-Imperial Africa at War," *Current History*, ibid., pp. 202 – 207.

64. "Image of A Country 'Tingling Back to Life': Everyone in Rwanda Has A Story of the Genocide Five Years Ago....," *The Christian Science Monitor*, April 9, 1999, p. 7.

65. "Bishop Seized by Rwanda in Massacres," op. cit.

66. Pasteur Bizimungu, ibid.

67. Quoted in "Catholic Clergy on Trial in Rwanda: For the First Time in History, A Catholic Bishop is Charged with Genocide," *The Christian Science Monitor*, September 21, 1999, p. 8; "State vs. Church: Rwanda Tribunal Tries Bishop for '94 Genocide," *International Herald Tribune*, October 1, 1999, p. 4:

"Before being taken to the killing ground where he now works as a tour guide, Emmanuel Murangira sought refuge at a church. It was April 1994, and as Hutu extremists swept through the countryside hunting

Rwanda's Tutsi minority, many were clamoring for refuge in the Roman Catholic churches that sit atop the country's lush green hills like crowns.

Mr. Murangira joined the thousands at the elegant compound of Bishop Augustin Misago, head of the Gikongoro diocese....But Bishop Misago told the terrified arrivals they must move on, sending them to the nearby classrooms of a technical college that today is a memorial filled with the smell of formaldehyde and the mummified corpses of 2,700 children, women, and men. That is a fraction of the thousands slaughtered there on the night of April 19, 1994.

'We went to Misago's place, and they brought us here,' said Mr. Murangira, a gaunt figure with a perfectly round depression above his left eye, the entrance wound of the bullet that punctured his brain. 'He was with the government and supported the killing here'....Bishop Misago, a Hutu, is the highest church official accused of helping to organize the genocide."

68. "Bishop Seized by Rwanda in Massacres," op. cit.; "Rwanda: Vatican on Bishop," *The New York Times*, April 16, 1999, p. A-8.

69. Aloys Habimana, quoted in "Massacres of '94: Rwanda Seeks Justice in Villages: Local Councils, Not the Overburdened Courts, May Rule on Guilt or Innocence," *The New York Times*, April 21, 1999, p. A-3.

70. Rwanda's Roman Catholic bishops, in a statement, quoted, ibid.

71. Azalyas Rukizangabo, ibid.

72. Abbey Alphonse Mazimpaka, ibid.

73. Jean de Dieu Mucyo, ibid.

74. Roger Rosenblatt, "Misplaced Tears: The Danger of Sympathy," *The New Republic*, May 10, 1999, pp. 18, and 19.

75. "Rwanda: 2 Sentenced in Genocide," *The New York Times*, June 4, 1999, p. A-6.

76. "Rwanda: 25 Sentenced in Genocide," *The New York Times*, July 3, 1999, p. A-4.

77. *World Press: News and Views From Around the World*, June 1999, p. 20; Baptiste Kayigamba, Inter Press Service, Rome, June 1999; Daniel Licht, in *Libération*, Paris, June 1999; *Golias*, Lyons, France, June 1999.

78. Gérard Chabon, quoted in *World Press*, ibid.; and in *Liberation*, June 1999.

79. "Rwanda Attempts an Atonement," *The Christian Science Monitor*, August 5, 1999, p. 5.

80. "Taming the Desire for Revenge: African Nations Draw on Cultural Heritage to Heal Wounds of War and Restore Social Fabric," *The Christian Science Monitor*, November 4, 1999, p. 15.

81. Michael Chege, "Africa's Murderous Professors," *The National Interest*, Washington, D.C., No. 46, Winter 1996/97, p. 34; *Kangura*, Gisenyi, Rwanda, 1993 – 1994; Gérard Prunier, *The Rwanda Crisis: History of A Genocide* (New York: Columbia University Press, 1995).

82. "Rwanda Testimony Set Today: Ex-UN Monitor Scheduled to Give His Version of Plot," *The Boston Globe*, February 23, 1998, p. A-2.

83. Romeo Dallaire, quoted in "UN General Tells Rwanda Panel of Anguish at Killings," The Boston Globe, February 26, 1998, p. A-2.

84. Charles Paul Freund, "The Atrocity Exhibition: A War Fueled by Imagery," *Reason: Free Minds and Free Markets*, Los Angeles, California, June 1999, p. 46.

85. R. Dallaire, cited in *Current History: A Journal of Contemporary World Affairs*, April 1998, p. 189; "Rwanda Massacres Were Avoidable, General Says," *The Christian Science Monitor*, February 27, 1998, p. 7.

86. "Rwanda Massacres Were Avoidable, General Says," ibid.

87. R. Dallaire, ibid.

88. "Echo of 1994 Genocide: Rwanda Slayings Persist," *The Christian Science Monitor*, March 3, 1998, p.

7.

89. Scot Straus, ibid.

90. Kingsley Moghalu, quoted in "One for the Law Books: In Africa, a UN Court Prosecutes Genocide – Tribunal in Arusha, Tanzania, Hopes to Set a Precedent in International Law," *The Christian Science Monitor*, March 4, 1998, p. 8.

91. Ibid.

92. Laity Kama, ibid.

93. Pascal Besnier, ibid.

94. Betty Murungi, ibid.

95. Ibid.

96. Bernard Ntuyahaga, in "Rwanda Panel Frees Suspect in Belgian Killings," *International Herald Tribune*, March 19, 1999, p. 2.

97. "Rwanda: Belgium Seeks Extradition," *The New York Times*, March 20, 1999, p. A-6.

98. Keith B. Richburg, *Out of America: A Black Man Confronts Africa* (New York: Basic Books, HarperCollins, 1997), pp. 96 – 97. See also George B.N. Ayittey, *Africa Betrayed* (New York: St. Martin's Press, 1992); G.B.N. Ayittey, *Africa in Chaos* (New York: St. Martin's Press, 1998).

99. Josephine Murebwayire, quoted in "Clinton Concedes US Erred in Rwanda: Cites Inadequate Response to Killing, Calls it Genocide," *The Boston Globe*, March 26, 1998, p. A-1.

100. Venuste Karasira, ibid.

101. Bill Clinton, ibid., pp. A-1, and A-20.

102. Gloriosa Uwimpuhwe, ibid., A-20.

103. "A New Piece to the Rwandan Puzzle: Belgian Contradicts French on Downing That Triggered Genocide," *International Herald Tribune*, April 8, 1998, p. 6. See also "French Accuse Uganda Over Missiles That Led to Massacres in Rwanda," *International Herald Tribune*, April 7, 1998, p. 7; "French Arsenal Tied to Downing of Africa Plane: 1994 Raid Led to Rwanda-

Burundi Strife," *The Boston Globe*, April 1, 1998, p. A-4; "French Leaders From '94 Defend Rwanda Policy: Charges of Complicity in Killings Are 'Revolting,' Balladur Asserts," *International Herald Tribune*, April 22, 1998, pp. 1, and 7; "Son Says Mitterand Tried to Promote Democracy in Rwanda," *International Herald Tribune*, April 23, 1998, p. 4.

104. Pasteur Bizimungu, quoted in "Rwanda Asks World to Prosecute Killers," *International Herald Tribune*, April 9, 1998, p. 4.

105. Yael S. Aronoff, "Clinton's Rwanda Apology is Fine, but America Needs to Act," *International Herald Tribune*, April 10, 1998, p. 8, and in *The Washington Post*, April 10, 1998. See also "French Panel Faults U.S. For Failure to Act in Rwanda," *International Herald Tribune*, December 16, 1998, p. 2:

"A French parliamentary commission concluded Tuesday (December 15) that the responsibility for preventing the genocide lay mainly in a United States-influenced failure of international will....Most of the inaction in Rwanda was the fault of the United Nations and its strongest member (the United States)....

The report said that the international community's 'passivity and inertia are due, among other reasons, to the hasty departure of the...Belgian-led UN contingent...after the assassination of 10 of its members and especially to the refusal of the United States to consider, after its debacle in Somalia, any immediate expansion of the UN force or any modification of its mandate to allow it to intervene."

106. James Woods, cited in "We Could Have Saved Rwandans," *International Herald Tribune*, January 29, 1999, p. 6; and *The Washington Post*, January 29, 1999.

107. Tony Marley, ibid.

108. Jean Kambanda, in *The Christian Science*

Monitor, May 5 1998, p. 2; *Current History: A Journal of Contemporary World Affairs,* September 1998, p. 287.

109. Kofi Annan, in *The Christian Science Monitor,* May 4, 1998, p. 2; *The New Yorker,* May 1998.

110. "Annan Reportedly Was Tipped on Killings," *The Boston Globe,* May 4, 1998, p. 2; *The New Yorker,* ibid.

111. Kofi Annan, in *The Christian Science Monitor,* May 5, 1998, p. 2.

112. K.Annan, "Annan Rejects Accusation of Failing to Act on Rwanda," *International Herald Tribune,* May 6, 1998, p. 2; *The New York Times,* May 6, 1998.

113. Ibid.; *Daily Nation,* and *The Standard,* Nairobi, Kenya, May 5, 1998; *Daily News,* Dar es Salaam, Tanzania, May 5, 1998.

114. K. Annan, in "Rwandan Tribunal Wins Annan Praise," *The Boston Globe,* May 6, 1998, p. A-15.

115. Anatole Nsengiyumya, ibid.

116. Joseph Bideri, quoted in "Rwanda, Anger at Annan: UN Chief is Snubbed, Blamed for 1994 Genocide," *The Boston Globe,* May 8, 1998, p. A-1.

117. K. Annan.

118. J. Bideri, ibid., p. A-24.

119. Anastase Gasana, ibid.

120. K. Annan, ibid.

121. Ibid.

122. Fred Eckhard, ibid.

123. Statement by Ibuka, an organization of genocide survivors, to Kofi Annan, ibid.

124. "Annan Takes the Rap in Rwanda: UN Chief Protects West for its Inaction During Genocide," *The New York Times,* May 9, 1998; and in the *International Herald Tribune,* May 9, 1998, p. 2.

125. Alain Destexhe, quoted in "The Rwanda Cable," in the *International Herald Tribune,* May 11, 1998, p. 10; and in *The Washington Post,* National Weekly Edition, May 18, 1998, p. 25.

126. For comparative analysis, see Telford Taylor,

Nuremberg and Vietnam (New York: Quadrangle Books, 1970), *Courts of Terror* (New York: Alfred A. Knopf, 1976), *Munich: The Price of Peace: The Definitive Account of the Fateful Conference of 1938* (New York: Doubleday,1979), among other works. See also "Telford Taylor, Nuremberg Prosecutor, Dies at 90," *International Herald Tribune*, May 25, 1998, p. 6:

"Telford Taylor, 90, a principal prosecutor of high Nazi officials and leading German industrialists at the Nuremberg war crimes trials after World War II, died of a stroke Saturday (May 23) in New York.

As a young army colonel at Nuremberg in 1945, Mr. Taylor helped write the rules for prosecuting Hermann Goering, Rudolph Hess and other top Nazis. He went on to become the trials' chief prosecutor and an authority on the laws of war.

In the decades after the Nuremberg trials, Mr. Taylor wrote and lectured extensively on the moral conduct of the United States and other nations and was an early opponent of Senator Joseph McCarthy. And the concerns that beckoned him was what he was as a continued reliance on war as an instrument of national policy and the commission of war crimes by the United States in Vietnam.

He began at the Nuremberg trials as an assistant to the chief counsel, the former U.S. Attorney General Robert Jackson. Mr. Jackson was the principal prosecutor leading Britain, France and the Soviet Union, as well as the United States, in the trials of Nazi leaders accused of crimes against humanity. Some Nazis were tried in local courts all over Europe as countries began to be liberated. But as the war drew to a close, the Americans felt strongly that there should be an international tribunal made up of representatives of the four major Allies.

In defining the proceedings, Mr. Taylor and Mr. Jackson agreed that even in the valuation of the people who had a role in creating death camps, conducting 'experiments' on unwilling subjects and securing slave labor for the war effort, there could be gradations of guilt.

Mr. Taylor disclosed nearly 50 years after the war, in his book *Anatomy of the Nuremberg Trials* (1992), that before he became involved in the trials, he was, like most Americans, ignorant of the mass extermination camps.

The initial indictments against 22 top Nazis resulted in 19 convictions; 12 Nazis were condemned to death, including Goering, chief of the Luftwaffe. But Goering committed suicide by taking poison in his cell before he could be executed.

In 1946, when Mr. Jackson left the prosecutor's post, Mr. Taylor was...named to succeed him. He soon won indictments against 23 German doctors and scientists, some of whom had conducted brutal experiments on prisoners of war. The second round of trials lasted until 1949 and was something of a disappointment to Mr. Taylor. Alfred Krupp, the main fabricator of large-caliber artillery, armor plate, submarines and warships for Hitler's war effort, and the directors of the I.G. Farben Chemical Co. were all acquitted of war crimes, like using slave labor, for lack of evidence.

If the results were not all that Mr. Taylor wanted, he believed that the war crimes trials had been successful, if for no other reason than to give the concept of 'crime against peace' precedent and legal standing."

The International Criminal Tribunal for Rwanda (ICTR) in Arusha, Tanzania, owes much of its existence to the work and legal precedents set at the Nuremberg trials. And its rulings may help to create a legal framework for the establishment of a permanent international war crimes tribunal under UN auspices to adjudicate cases from all countries – provided there is the political will, among all UN members, to establish such a court; a remote possibility.

127. *Current History: A Journal of Contemporary World Affairs*, September 1999, p. 298.

128. Agwu Okiwe Okali, quoted in "Rwanda Tribunal Puts Out Call for Help," *International Herald Tribune*, May 25, 1998, p. 6; and in *The New York Times*, May 25, 1998.

129. Ibid.

130. "Rwanda Tribunal Puts Out Call for Help," ibid.

131. Herman Cohen, quoted in "Former Aide Says U.S. Was Wrong on Rwanda," *International Herald Tribune*, July 9, 1998, p. 6.

132. Ibid.

133. "For U.S. Protégé in Rwandan Army, What Use Was Rights Training?," *International Herald Tribune*, July 15, 1998, p. 10.

134. Diplomat in Kigali, Rwanda, quoted, ibid.

135. "UN Tribunal on Rwanda to Deliver Verdict," *The Boston Globe*, September 2, 1998, p. A-2.

136. Laity Kama, quoted in "Rwandan Ex-Premier Imprisoned for Life," *The Boston Globe*, September 5, 1998, p. A-4.

137. Alice Karekezi, ibid.

138. Nicholas Taingaye, ibid.

139. Pierre Prosper, ibid.

140. K. Annan, ibid.

141. Faiza Jama Mohammed, ibid.

142. K. Annan, quoted in "Genocide Trial Verdict: Guilty. Tribunal Convicts Rwandan Official of Masterminding Tutsi Slaughter," *The Boston Globe*, September 3, 1998, p. A-2.

143. Binaifer Nowrogee, ibid.

144. Jean-Paul Akayesu, ibid.

145. Patrick Mazimhaka, ibid.

146. Michael Inglis, defence lawyer for Jean Kambanda, quoted, ibid.

147. Ibid.

148. Laity Kama, quoted in "Ex-Rwanda Mayor

Sentenced to Life in Genocide," *The Boston Globe*, October 3, 1998, p. A-2.

149. Ibid.

150. Ibid.

151. L. Kama, quoted in "Rwanda Mayor Gets 3 Life Terms for Genocide," *International Herald Tribune*, October 3, 1998, p. 5.

152. Ibid.

153. Kingsley Chiedu Moghalu, "Rwanda Panel's Legacy: They Can Run But Not Hide," *International Herald Tribune*, October 31, 1998, p. 6; *Los Angeles Times*, October 31, 1998.

154. Prosecution indictment against Omar Serushago, International Criminal Tribunal for Rwanda (ICTR), Arusha, Tanzania, quoted in "Rwandan Militia Leader Admits to Genocide and Related Crimes," *International Herald Tribune*, December 15, 1998, p. 2. See also, Omar Serushago, in *Keesing's Record of World Events*, December 1998, p. 42660; and pp. 41720 – 21, and 42254.

155. "Rwanda: Kenya Holds War Crimes Suspects," *The New York Times*, February 20, 1999, p. A-5.

156. "Rwanda: Genocide Suspect Freed," *The New York Times*, March 19, 1999, p. A-6. See also "UN Council Backs Inquiry on Rwanda," *International Herald Tribune*, March 27, 1999, p. 2.

157. "Rwanda: Officer Tied to Killings Freed," *The New York Times*, March 30, 1999, p. A-6.

158. Bernard Ntuyahaga, in the *International Herald Tribune*, March 31, 1999, p. 7.

159. "Tanzania: Rwandan Arrested," *The New York Times*, March 31, 1999, p. A-6.

160. "Rwanda: 3 Ex-Aides Charged in Slayings," *The New York Times*, April 8, 1999, p. A-6.

161. "War Crimes Trial for Ex-Mayor," *The New York Times*, April 13, 1999, p. A-8.

162. "Rwanda: Two Convicted of Genocide," *The New York Times*, May 22, 1999, p. A-4.

163. "Rwanda's International Tribunal: Group Trials," *The Economist*, May 21, 1999, p. 36.

164. Joseph Mutaboba, commenting on the release of Jean-Bosco Barayagwiza – one of the most notorious perpetrators of the 1994 Rwandan genocide – on a legal technicality, quoted in "Rwanda Halts Support of UN Tribunal," *International Herald Tribune*, November 13, 1999, p. 4; and in *The New York Times*, November 13, 1999.

165. Zephyr Mutanguha, quoted in "Rwanda Denies Visa to UN Prosecutor," *International Herald Tribune*, November 23, 1999, p. 4.

166. Ibid.; "Rwanda-Genocide Court Delays Release of Suspect," *International Herald Tribune*, November 29, 1999, p. 4; *The New York Times*, November 29, 1999.

167. Georges Rutuganda, in "Rwandan Given Life for Tutsi Genocide," *International Herald Tribune*, December 7, 1999, p. 10.

168. Laity Kama, ibid.

169. Novanethem Pillay, quoted in "Order to Release Suspect Puts Court in a Bind: Rwandan Genocide Trial in Crisis – 'Integrity of Tribunal is at Stake'," *International Herald Tribune*, December 20, 1999, p. 2; *The New York Times*, December 20, 1999.

170. "Order to Release Suspect Puts Court in a Bind," ibid.

171. Joseph Mutaboba, quoted in "Rwanda Halts Support of UN Tribunal," op. cit.

172. Ruling by the Appeals Chamber, at The Hague, on Jean-Bosco Barayagwiza's case before the international war crimes tribunal in Arusha, Tanzania, quoted in "Order to Release Suspect Puts Court in a Bind," op. cit.

173. Richard Sezibera, ibid.

174. "At Stake: Credibility of War Crimes Tribunal – Appeals Court Reconsiders Its Decision to Free Rwandan Accused of Genocide," *The Christian Science Monitor*, February 24, 2000, p. 7. See also, Jean-Bosco

Barayagwiza, in *Current History: A Journal of Contemporary World Affairs*, May 2000, p. 233:

"International Tribunal for War Crimes in Rwanda, March 31, 2000 – The Tanzania-based body's appeals court reverse(d) a November (1999) decision by the tribunal to free genocide suspect Jean-Bosco Barayagwiza. The initial decision, made on the grounds that Barayagwiza had been jailed for over 2 years without being charged with a specific crime, outraged Rwandan officials and nearly led to a halt to the tribunal's work."

175. Elizaphan Ntakirutimana, in "Rwanda: Sent Back to Answer for a Massacre," Newsweek, March 13, 2000, p. 4.

176. Kofi Annan, in "UN Bungled Intervention in Rwanda, Inquiry Says: Panel Criticizes Weak and Slow Response of World Body and U.S.," *International Herald Tribune*, December 17, 1999, p. 1; and in *The New York Times*, December 17, 1999, p. A-1.

177. Ingvar Carlsson, ibid.

178. Report by a panel that investigated the UN failure to intervene in Rwanda, quoted, ibid.

179. bid.

180. "UN Bungled Intervention in Rwanda, Inquiry Says," ibid.

181. "Looking Back at Rwanda," *The New York Times*, December 18, 1999; and *International Herald Tribune*, December 18, 1999, p. 6.

182. "Rwanda Revisited: A Look at the Biggest Bloodstain on the World's Conscience in the 1990s," *The Economist*, December 31, 1999, pp. 5 – 6.

183. "Confession on Rwanda," editorial, in *The Washington Post*, December 21, 1999; and in the *International Herald Tribune*, December 21, 1999, p. 4. See also, "Strange Justice: The World Betrays Rwanda Again," on the release of Jean-Bosco Barayagwiza who

was arrested in Cameroon in March 1996 but was not transferred to the UN war crimes tribunal in Tanzania until November 1997, in *The New Republic*, Washington, D.C., December 20, 1999, p. 11.

For a comprehensive survey of the UN peacekeeping role in conflicts around the world, see William Shawcross, *Deliver Us From Evil: Peacekeepers, Warlords and a World of Endless Conflict* (New York: Simon & Schuster, 2000).

However, Shawcross' work is also hagiographic, especially about UN Secretary-General Kofi Annan. For a contrasting view, see David Rieff's review and critique of Shawcross' book, "Nothing Was Delivered," *The New Republic*, May 1, 2000, pp. 26 – 33.

See also, *Report of the Independent Inquiry into the Actions of the United Nations During the 1994 Genocide in Rwanda*, United Nations Document, New York, December 15, 1999; Michael Ignatieff, "The Next President's Duty to Intervene," *The New York Times*, February 13, 2000, in which he discusses the responsibility of the key country, the United States, to intervene in crises to stop genocide and avert other catastrophes when preventive diplomacy fails.

See also, Philip Gourevitch, "Crimes Against Humanity Persist on UN Watch," *The Wall Street Journal*, December 22, 1999, criticism of Kofi Annan who was chief of the UN peacekeeping operations during the Rwandan genocide, for his dereliction of duty before and during the holocaust. Annan contended otherwise; so did his supporters, including Brian Urquhart who stated in his article, "In the Name of Humanity," in *The New York Review of Books*, April 27, 2000, p. 20:

"Kofi Annan, who was then head of the UN's peacekeeping department, in vain approached about one hundred governments seeking troops for Rwanda. He

220

agreed with (General Romeo) Dallaire that with five thousand UN troops, hundreds of thousands of lives could have been saved, but, he said in 1998, 'the will to provide men, the will to act, was not there.'

The UN Secretariat, for its part, contributed to the disaster by failing to take any effective action in response to an authoritative and detailed warning of the plans for the genocide, which it had received three months before it started." See also pp. 19 – 22, ibid.

For more insight into the dynamics of ethno-politics and nationalism in Rwanda and Burundi and other countries, see:

Karl Deutsch, *Nationalism and Its Alternative* (New York: Alfred A. Knopf, 1969); Hylland Thomas Eriksen, *Ethnicity and Nationalism: Anthropological Perspectives* (London: Pluto Press, 1993); Robert Ted Gurr and Barbara Harff, *Ethnic Conflict in World Politics* (Boulder, Colorado, USA: Westview Press, 1994); Ian Linden, *Church and Revolution in Rwanda* (Manchester, UK, and New York: Manchester University Press, 1977); Liisa Malkki, *Purity and Exile: Violence, Memory, and National Cosmology among Hutu Refugees in Tanzania* (Chicago: University of Chicago Press, 1995).

Thomas Malady, *Burundi: The Tragic Years* (Maryknoll, New York: Orbis Books, 1974); Daniel Patrick Moynihan, *Pandaemonium: Ethnicity in International Politics* (Oxford: Oxford University Press, 1993); Manning Nash, *The Cauldron of Ethnicity in the Modern World* (Chicago: University of Chicago Press, 1989); David Ress, *The Burundi Ethnic Massacres: 1988* (San Francisco: Mellon Research University Press, 1988); Pierre van de Berghe, *The Ethnic Phenomenon* (New York: Praeger, 1987); Catherine Watson, *Exile from Rwanda: Background to an Invasion* (Washington, D.C.: American Council for Nationalities Service, 1991).

John Webster, *The Political Development of Rwanda*

221

and Burundi (Syracuse, New York: Syracuse University Press, 1966); Warren Weinstein and Robert Schrire, *Political Conflict and Ethnic Strategies: A Case Study of Burundi* (Syracuse, New York: Maxwell School of Citizenship and Public Affairs, Syracuse University Press, 1976); Milton Yinger, *Ethnicity: Source of Strength? Source of Conflict?* (Albany, New York: State University of New York Press, 1994); Wole Soyinka, *The Open Sore of a Continent: A Personal Narrative of the Nigerian Crisis* (New York: Oxford University Press, 1996); W. Soyinka, *The Burden of Memory, The Muse of Forgiveness* (New York: Oxford University Press, 1999).

For comparative study, see also Stephen Ellis, *The Mask of Anarchy: The Destruction of Liberia and the Religious Dimension of an African Civil War* (New York: New York University Press, 2000); Daniel Jonah Goldhagen, *Hitler's Willing Executioners: Ordinary Germans and the Holocaust* (New York: Alfred A. Knopf, 1997).

Part Two

1. Chukwuemeka Odumegwu Ojukwu, "Statement by Lieutenant-Colonel Ojukwu," 5 August 1968, in *Africa Contemporary Record: Annual Survey and Documents 1968 – 1969* (London: Africa Research Ltd., 1969), p. 654.

2. Ibid.

3. Anthony Enahoro, "Chief Enahoro's Statement," in *Africa contemporary Record,* ibid., p. 673.

4. Bertrand Rusell, quoted by Frank Smyth, "The Horror-Rwanda: A History Lesson," *The New Republic,* Washington, D.C., June 20, 1994, p. 19. See also Neil J. Kressel, *Mass Hate: The Global Rise of Genocide and Terror* (New York: Plenum Press, 1996), p. 100.

5. Manifesto *of the Bahutu: A Note on the Social Aspects of the Indigenous Racial Problem in Rwanda,*

Kigali, Rwanda, March 1957.

6. Catherine Newbury, *The Cohesion of Oppression: Clientship and Ethnicity in Rwanda: 1860 – 1890* (New York: Columbia University Press, 1988); Jack David Eller, *From Culture to Ethnicity to Conflict: An Anthropological Perspective on Ethnic Conflict* (Ann Arbor: University of Michigan Press, 1999), p. 221. See also J.D. Eller, ibid., chap. 5: "Rwanda and Burundi: When Two Tribes Go to War?," pp. 195 – 241.

7. A statement issued by conservative Tutsi chiefs, quoted in John Webster, *The Political Development of Rwanda and Burundi* (Syracuse, New York: Syracuse University Press, 1966), p. 43.

8. Quoted in René Lemarchand, *Rwanda and Burundi* (New York: Frederick A. Praeger, 1970), p. 161.

9. United Nations Commission for Ruanda-Urundi, March 1961 report, quoted in R. Lemarchand, *Rwanda and Burundi*, ibid., pp. 194 – 195. See also John Reader, *Africa: A Biography of the Continent* (New York: Alfred A. Knopf, 1998), pp. 617 – 621, 633 – 636 – 671 – 679.

10. J.D. Eller, *From Culture to Ethnicity to Conflict*, op. cit., p. 224. See also Alan J. Kuperman, "Rwanda in Retrospect," *Foreign Affairs*, January/February 2000, p. 94: "During the transition to independence starting in 1959, the Hutu seized control in a violent struggle that spurred the exodus of about half the Tutsi population to neighboring states."

11. René Lemarchand, "Burundi," in R. Lemarchand, editor, *African Kingships in Perspective: Political Change and Modernization in Monarchical Settings* (London: Frank Cass, 1977), pp. 93 – 126.

12. Warren Weistein and Robert Schrire, *Political Conflict and Ethnic Strategies: A Case Study of Burundi* (Syracuse, New York: Maxwell School of Citizenship and Public Affairs, Syracuse University Press, 1976), p. 15; René Lemarchand, "The Fire in the Great Lakes," *Current History: A Journal of Contemporary World Affairs, Vol.*

98, No. 628, Philadelphia, Pennsylvania, USA, May 1999, pp. 197 – 198:

"Although many Hutu politicians in Burundi looked to republican Rwanda as their model, the main vector of conflict was the tens of thousands of Tutsi refugees who had streamed into the country in the wake of the revolution next door. Nothing could have done more to alert Burundi's Tutsis to the Hutu danger than the tales of horror and destruction to which their Rwandan counterparts bore witness. With Rwanda under Hutu control, Burundi became the mirror image of its neighbor to the north, with the Tutsis assuming a quasi-hegemonic position in the government and the army." See also R. Lemarchand, *Burundi: Ethnic Conflict and Genocide* (New York: Cambridge University Press, 1996).

13. Catharine Watson, *Exile from Rwanda: Background to an Invasion* (Washington, D.C.: American Council for Nationalities Service, 1991), p. 5; J.D. Eller, *From Culture to Ethnicity to Conflict*, op. cit., p. 233.

14. Thomas Melady, *Burundi: The Tragic Years* (Maryknoll, New York: Orbis Books, 1974), pp. 4, and 11.

15. N. J. Kressel, *Mass Hate: The Global Rise of Genocide and Terror*, op. cit., p. 102. See also chap. 4: "Rwanda – The Legacy of Inequality," pp. 87 – 118.

16. Ibid., pp. 102 – 103. See also Stanley Meisler, "Holocaust in Burundi, 1972," in Frank Chalk and Kurt Jonassohn, editors, *The History and Sociology of Genocide* (New Haven, Connecticut: Yale University Press, 1990), pp. 384 – 393; Leo Kuper, *Genocide: Its Political Use in the Twentieth Century* (New Haven, Connecticut: Yale University Press, 1981), p. 63.

17. T. Melady, *Burundi: The Tragic Years*, op. cit., pp. 25 – 26.

18. J.D. Eller, *From Culture to Ethnicity to Conflict*, op. cit., p. 235.

19. René Lemarchand, *Burundi: Ethnocide as*

Discourse and Practice (Cambridge: Cambridge University Press, 1994), p. 98.

20. Jerry Gray, "2 Nations Joined by Common History of Genocide," *The New York Times*, April 9, 1994, p. A-6.

21. Hutu People's Liberation Party (PALIPEHUTU), in one of its pamphlets, quoted in David Reiss, *The Burundi Ethnic Massacre* (San Francisco, California: Mellon Research University Press, 1988), p. 97.

22. Pierre Buyoya, quoted in D. Reiss, *The Burundi Ethnic Massacres*, ibid., p. 114.

23. "Rwandan President Resigns," *The Christian Science Monitor*, March 24, 2000, p. 24. The Rwandan Patriotic Front (RPF) appointed Paul Kagame as president and said his term would end in 2003, according to "Africa News: Nightline Africa," Voice of America (VOA), Washington, D.C., April 1, 2000.

24. Pasteur Bizimungu, cited by "Africa News: Nightline Africa," Voice of America (VOA), March 26, 2000.

25. "Resignations Put Rwanda's 'Unity' Rule in Jeopardy," The Christian Science Monitor, March 27, 2000, pp. 7, and 24.

See also George B.N. Ayittey, *Africa in Chaos* (New York: St. Martin's Press, 1998); Godfrey Mwakikagile, *The Modern African State: Quest for Transformation* (Huntington, New York: Nova Science Publishers, Inc., 2001); human Rights Watch, *Proxy Targets: Civilians in the War in Burundi* (New York: Human Rights Watch, 1998), and *Leave None to Tell the Story: Genocide in Rwanda* (New York: Human Rights Watch, 1999).

Appendix I:

The Tutsi And Hutu
Need a Partition

Makau wa Mutua
The New York Times
August 30, 2000

This week President Clinton went to Arusha, Tanzania, hoping to witness the signing of a peace agreement ending the genocidal war in Burundi. All too predictably -- and despite the tireless efforts of Nelson Mandela as a mediator -- the only agreement that Burundi's Hutu and Tutsi ethnic groups could agree on was essentially meaningless, failing to provide for any genuine sharing of power.

Mr. Clinton's public support for Mr. Mandela's unenviable task in Burundi is a wasted symbolic gesture,

227

squandering the prestige of the United States, just as the mediation effort itself squanders Mr. Mandela's mythic abilities. Both men should realize that a democratic renewal of central Africa is not possible unless the Hutu-Tutsi problem is resolved.

The boilerplate approach to diplomacy in civil conflicts -- an emphasis on power sharing between hostile groups and a transition to real democracy -- is hopeless in this case. Rather than trying to force the Hutu and the Tutsi to live together, Mr. Mandela ought to openly voice the belief of most ordinary Africans: that peace cannot come to Burundi or neighboring Rwanda unless the Hutu and Tutsi are separated by an international border.

Burundi and Rwanda are dysfunctional states created by old colonial borders. The Tutsi, who constitute only 15 percent of the population in both countries but control the governments and the armies, will absolutely not permit genuine democracy because the Hutu, with their 85 per cent majorities, would dominate any free and fair elections.

Burundi's flirtation with experimental democracy in 1993 ended when the Tutsi-dominated military overthrew and killed the Hutu president after he had been in office five months. In Rwanda, the first-ever Hutu government carried out the orchestrated genocide of 1994, in which over half a million Tutsi were killed.

Nor would power-sharing arrangements, or giving the Hutu some sort of autonomy within each country, be realistic. The Tutsi governments have vowed that they will never give up any part of the state or allow a Hutu majority in the army. Hutu and Tutsi in both countries see the exclusive control of the state as an essential precondition to their survival as a people.

Redrawing the map of central Africa may seem radical, but consider what has happened elsewhere since the end of the cold war. The Soviet Union was broken up largely along ethnic and cultural lines (the war in Chechnya is an

228

example of what can happen when non-Russian people are kept under Moscow's rule). The conflicts in the former Yugoslavia have been quelled only when lines have been drawn to divide ethnic groups or armed troops keep the peace.

Just like Kosovar Albanians and Serbs, the Tutsi and the Hutu cannot live together or tolerate each other. The differences between the two groups are not linguistic, cultural or racial; the division is simply about power. Over the centuries, caste and status solidified identities, with the Tutsi emerging as rulers. Belgian colonial rule further entrenched and distorted Tutsi domination, creating the ineradicable hatreds that have exploded in the last decade into gruesome atrocities.

Now all of Central Africa is affected. Since 1998, troops from Rwanda, Uganda and Burundi have supported an insurgency to overthrow President Laurent Kabila of Congo largely because of his failure to curb attacks on the Rwandan government by Hutu operating out of eastern Congo. Zimbabwe, Namibia, Chad and Angola have sent troops into Congo to support Mr. Kabila.

A real solution to the Hutu-Tutsi conflict -- and the Congo war -- would be for a United Nations panel to redraw the maps of Burundi and Rwanda to create two wholly new states: one for the Hutu, the other for the Tutsi. Mr. Mandela's imprimatur on such a proposal would instantly legitimize it in Africa -- and within the Clinton administration. The logistics of such a plan may seem daunting, but in the end it would be far better to conduct large population transfers now than to accept genocide every few years.

Appendix II:

Redraw Colonial Borders to Quell the Frenzy

Ali A. Mazrui,
Los Angeles Times
November 13, 1996

ACCRA, Ghana — The crisis in eastern Zaire and between Zaire and its neighbors poses the greatest challenge yet to the artificial borders that imperial European powers drew at the turn of the century to create the current so-called "nation-states" in Africa. It has taken a Tutsi-trigger to spark an agonizing reappraisal.

The longer-term scenario emerging from the crisis may be the gradual redefining of the boundaries between Zaire, Rwanda and Burundi. Because the European partition of Africa in the 19th and 20th centuries made no attempt to make the country borders coincide with the borders of ethnic groups, each includes indigenous Hutu and Tutsi within its own borders. In the mid-1990s, after fluctuating fortunes, the Tutsi find themselves as having the upper hand in Burundi, Rwanda and now Zaire.

Is this the moment for making ethnic boundaries coincide with national boundaries? Are we seeing the tumultuous process of creating a Tutsi "Israel," an independent homeland for the Tutsi? Is a Tutsi-stan being born?

Until the mid-1980s, the Tutsis seemed to be the Kurds of eastern Africa, a marginalized minority in Rwanda, Zaire and under a different name (the Hima) in Uganda. Temporarily they clung desperately and brutally to power in Burundi. But as a minority, they seemed to be up against history. It was thought that in time they would become marginalized in Burundi also.

It was not until 1986 that the tide turned when Yoweri Museveni, ethnically linked to the people of Rwanda, captured power in Uganda. After Museveni's successful consolidation of his political base in Uganda, he turned to meet his obligation to the Rwandans by helping to train the Rwanda Patriotic Front.

In 1994, the RPF staged a successful "Bay of Pigs" operation from the Ugandan border. Like the Cuban exiles under Presidents Eisenhower and Kennedy, the Rwandan exiles had been trained by a neighboring country for a major military penetration of their own country. But unlike the Cuban effort of 1961, the Rwanda operation was completely successful. The Rwandan exiles from Uganda routed the Hutu and established an alternative government in Kigali.

This created a situation in which Hutu refugees in Zaire started plotting and training for a counteroffensive-- with secret support from Zaire itself and possibly from Kenya and France. To make matters worse, the Zairean security forces started picking on Zairean Tutsi, who had been part of Zaire since before the 19th century partition of Africa.

When Zairean Tutsi were threatened with expulsion from their homeland by Zairean armed forces, they formed an army of resistance (secretly supported by Rwanda) and turned out to be more than a match for the Zairean security forces. In their resistance, they have in fact threatened the integrity of the entire Zairean state. If these rebels can get away with their resistance in one part of the country, what is to stop political emulation in other parts of Zaire?

But what are the Tutsi going to do with their Hutu neighbors? The exchange of populations to create a separate Hutu state may be a prescription for future interstate wars, as the Arabs and Israelis and the Indians and Pakistanis have found to their detriment.

A more viable, longer term solution would be the federation of Rwanda, Burundi and Tanzania. The armies of Rwanda and Burundi would be pensioned off. In this larger political community, the Hutu and the Tutsi would discover how much they have in common culturally and might learn to be on the same political side on many issues in the enlarged Tanzania (just as their ethnic cousins in Uganda, the Hima and the Iru, often have voted on the same side against other groups in the larger national context of Uganda).

Burundi